Boy Bands Are Back!

In today's music scene, boy bands dominate the air-waves with their hot dance hits and soulful ballads. They're even branching out into television and movies. On the way to the top they've proved their critics wrong—these guy groups have won the respect of their peers, and they won't disappear any time soon. Get the inside scoop on the young singing sensations who have conquered the pop world and find out what it really takes to succeed as a boy band.

Including all-new interviews with some of the best boy bands and biggest industry insiders, plus eight pages of color photos, only one book has the behind-the-scenes stories of today's hottest music groups . . .

The Ultimate Boy Band Book

Look for other music biographies from
Archway Paperbacks

the Ultimate BOY BAND BOOK

Frederick Levy

AN ARCHWAY PAPERBACK
Published by POCKET BOOKS
New York   London   Toronto   Sydney   Singapore

AN ARCHWAY PAPERBACK *Original*

An Archway Paperback published by
POCKET BOOKS, a division of Simon & Schuster, Inc.
1230 Avenue of the Americas, New York, NY 10020

Copyright © 2000 by Frederick Levy

All rights reserved, including the right to reproduce
this book or portions thereof in any form whatsoever.
For information address Pocket Books, 1230 Avenue
of the Americas, New York, NY 10020

ISBN: 0-7434-0669-9

First Archway Paperback printing September 2000

10 9 8 7 6 5 4 3 2

AN ARCHWAY PAPERBACK and colophon are
registered trademarks of Simon & Schuster, Inc.

Front cover photo credits, clockwise from top: Gene Shaw/Star File;
Bill Davila/Retna; Jeffrey Mayer/Star File

Printed in the U.S.A.

IL 4+

For my cousins,
Lyndsay and Samantha Schneiderman;
Shaina, Leah, and Chad Douty;
Tara and Ethan Levy; and Alex DesLauriers

And in honor of my best friend's wedding,
where Hilary and Nathan Cherniss first danced
as a married couple to Ronan Keating's
"When You Say Nothing At All"

Acknowledgments

This book never could have been written without the help and support of so many people. First and foremost, my agent, Andree Abecassis at the Ann Elmo Agency. What can I say, you've done it again? Also thanks to Lettie Lee.

To Tiffany Tiesiera, my incredible assistant, without you this book would never have been finished on time. Also, to my editors, Liz Shiflett and Lisa Clancy at Pocket Books, thank you for helping turn a good idea into a great book.

To those creative and talented performers who allowed me to examine them up close and personal and who granted me access to interview them for this book: BBMak (Christian Burns, Mark Barry, and Stephen McNally), C Note (Brody Martinez, Raul Molina, David Perez, and Dru Rogers), Howie Dorough, Justin Jeffre, Josh Keaton, Drew Lachey, Nick Lachey, Ricky Martin, Joey McIntyre, The Moffatts (Bob Moffatt, Clint Moffatt, Dave Moffatt, and Scott Moffatt), No Authority (Ricky G., Tommy McCarthy, Eric Stretch, and Danny Zavatsky), Plus One (Nate Cole, Gabe Combs, Jeremy Mhire, Jason Perry, and Nathan Walters), Wade Robson, Abel Talamantez, and Youngstown (James Dallas, Sammy Lopez, and David Yeager).

Acknowledgments

To the amazing professionals who work so hard behind the scenes and contribute so much to the success of these musical acts: Gary Baker, Mary-Ellis Bunim, Don Crabtree, Edgardo Diaz, Nigel Dick, "Bow Legged" Lou George and Full Force, Robin Jones, Lionel C. Martin, Jonathan Murray, Lou Pearlman, Fatima Robinson, Keith Stegall, JoJo Wright. Also thanks to Gregg Joumas and Dick Sittig.

And finally, for those who helped with the coordination of interviews, research, and access: Lexie Almeida, Starr Andreeff, *Billboard* magazine, Billboard Music Awards, Glen Blackman, Tonya Davies, Joel Dean, Jim DeFabritus, Melissa Dishell, Kathleen Finn, David Foster, Fox Television, Jim Gosnell, Mel Haber, Donavan Hebard, Fred Iberri, Nurul Ismail, Jerry Jaffe, Brian Jansen, Rick Joyce, KIIS-FM Los Angeles, Katy Krassner, James Krisel, LA Shanti, Fabrice Lechant, Jay Marose, Gregg McBride, William McLaughlin, Sinead Ni Mheallaigh, Mozelle Miley, Lizza Morales, Ray Prisby, Andy Putschoegl, Radio Disney, Cindy Ronzoni, Craig Scolthrup, Drew Tappin, John Tellem, Trans-Continental Entertainment, Michael Valeo, Robert Williams, and Diane Young.

Author's Note

The music world is constantly changing. I've tried to include the most up-to-date information about all the groups covered in this book at the time of printing. For the latest information on your favorite musical acts, and to hear about the newest boy bands on the block, check out this book's official World Wide Web site at www.boybandbook.com.

Throughout the book, various Web sites are listed to find out additional information about individual groups. The sites in this book are those that were on the Web as of this printing. Also, remember that people on the Internet are often not who they say they are, so never give your name or identifying information to anyone.

Now sit back, pop in your favorite CD, and enjoy the book!

Contents

Contents

The History of Boy Bands

Liverpool, 1957: a boy named John Lennon forms a band that lays the foundation for what is to become the most famous group of all time. By 1962 the band—including Paul McCartney, George Harrison, and Ringo Starr—evolves into what we've come to know as the Beatles, considered by many to be the first official boy band.

Beatlemania, the hype and excitement surrounding the band, began in 1963. The following year the supergroup conquered America. A media frenzy erupted over the group's every move. Screaming girls and admiring boys couldn't get enough of the Fab Four. No band had ever before received such a wild reception.

The Beatles phenomenon affected not only music, but style and fashion as well. The group single-handedly transformed the music industry and created one of the earliest forms of the music video called the Prop promo film.

"I was eleven years old when the Beatles came on the scene," recalls music-video director Nigel Dick, who specializes in teen music and directed the MTV boy-band spoof, *2gether*. "I was right there at the beginning of the boy bands."

The formula caught on and it hasn't stopped since. From the Beach Boys, the Monkees and the Jackson Five, to the Osmonds and Boyz II Men, boy bands have always held a special place in a young girl's heart.

Until now, the closest thing to Beatlemania occurred during the eighties with the success of teen group New Kids on the Block. Taking musical inspiration from R&B acts like New Edition, New Kids emerged as a major player in the music scene. But it was actually the Latin boy band Menudo that first breathed new life into the trend.

"Maurice Starr, producer of New Kids on the Block, traveled to Puerto Rico and he met with me, and a couple others who were part of the RCA team," recalls Edgardo Diaz, Menudo's founder. "The idea was that we were going to record an English album, and Maurice brings a couple songs and we said that's not what we're looking for. We want more pop music instead of R&B. We felt that the guys would not be able to sing that kind of music. They can't feel it the same way that other people, especially black singers, can. For that reason, we don't record anything with him. As I understand, Maurice went and made New Kids on the Block. He records the same songs that he showed us, but nothing happens and he changes direction to what we told him we wanted to do—pop music."

Menudo was one of the very first prefabricated bands, one that was manufactured by a management company. Up until then the boy bands had been self-formed. "When we were with Menudo, we were looking for kids whose talent we could develop. We can teach them," explains Diaz. "With Menudo I was looking for kids who I could look at and say 'We can make a star of him.' "

When the New Kids began, nobody took them seriously at first. In fact, their self-titled debut album was not successful at all. However, with the release of *Hangin' Tough* in 1988, the course of music history was changed yet again. The album spawned such memorable hits as "You Got It (The Right Stuff)," "Please Don't Go Girl," "I'll Be Loving You Forever," and of course, the album's title song. The record was so successful that the group's first album was actually rereleased the following year.

"When we first heard them sing, we were like 'Wow, these white boys can sing,'" recalls "Bow Legged" Lou George of songwriting/producing team Full Force. "I can't take away anything from New Kids on the Block because they're the ones that paved the way for all these boy bands today, for all these white boy bands anyway. I'd have to say Boyz II Men paved the way for the way that these boy bands are singing now."

Today's top boy bands are an evolution of everything past. They've got the look and the moves of the New Kids, the soul and the sound of Boyz II Men, and some are even writing their own material and playing live instruments like the Beatles. On top of that, in today's music industry, boy bands have become big business.

"It's ten years later. It's a new day. It's a new business," agrees former New Kid Joey McIntyre. "With Backstreet Boys, the record company knew what they were dealing with. They knew what they had and they knew what they had to do. They treated it like the Rolling Stones. Back in the day with the New Kids, granted, we were tied to Maurice Starr and he was gonna write the songs, so unfortunately we were a different gig. We didn't have eight of the best writers and producers in the world to do our next album. People realize how big a business it is now. We were sort of this capsule, this own little thing that just kind of happened. People didn't really know what it was, but now they know what it is and they know how to deal with it."

"Isn't it fun?" asks Robin Jones, program director for Radio Disney when asked about the current resurgence of boy bands. "I don't think it's a whole lot different from the Partridge Family, and the Osmonds, and the Jackson Five to be honest with you. It's kids that the kids can relate to. It helps that they're nice to look at."

"I'm happy that I can sit with Jermaine Jackson and we can exchange stories about being in boy bands and being a part of pop history," says Joey. "That's cool, that's humbling. We didn't invent that [stuff]. It's timeless. You put five guys together. It's the same as five guys on a corner just doing a doo-wop. It just happens that the right guy didn't drive by and find them."

The trend is one that obviously repeats itself through time. Boy bands will reach the height of popularity, play for a few years, and then fade once again into obscurity. But the dawn of the new millennium just seems so ripe for these kinds of acts.

"It's almost like the antithesis of rap to a certain degree if I may be as bold to say that," suggests songwriter Keith Stegall, who penned the song "I Do (Cherish You)" made popular by 98 Degrees. "There's a lot of love songs, very positive, very much about love and relationships. You always see trends of things that will happen. We just happen to be in that trend right now. I don't know how long it will last. Always when one successful thing happens, like a boy band, then of course everyone else starts looking for those types of things and realizing that there's a viable market out there and that people are getting into it. It's like anything else. It will be just a trend, though I hope it lasts for a while to be honest with you."

Songwriter Gary Baker, who has written songs for several of the guy groups including Backstreet Boys and Boyzone, says, "I think they've [young people] brought so much life into the music business, and a lot of money into it."

"This teen stuff isn't just driving the music business," an Elektra Records executive said to *Entertainment Weekly*. "It *is* the music business."

Deejay JoJo Wright of KIIS-FM, Los Angeles theorizes, "I guess it's because of a void in the market. Maybe young, mainstream girls were starved for a young clean-cut, modern-day version of the Beatles, cute guys on stage. There's a void in the market for . . . girls to fall in love with an Elvis or a New Kids on the Block. Although I think this overall explosion now is bigger than it was with the New Kids, I don't know if anybody is bigger than the New Kids."

Music-video director Lionel C. Martin adds, "I think it's history repeating itself. I think it's gonna last for a little while, but I think it's gonna be a cycle. It might go to some girl groups for a while. Then all of a sudden it's gonna go to something different. You can almost say that it's predictable. I think the one who wins in that game is the person who has his pulse, who can probably figure out when this cycle is gonna take place.

"I think it's the makeup of the market, Generation X," Martin continues. "I think parents feel good about these boy bands because they're not really controversial. I think the boy bands are real safe for America. My daughter loves 'N Sync—I feel safe. That's great. You don't feel threatened, you don't feel like they're gonna come home with some bad habits. So I think that's one of the things that's really appealing about these groups right now."

"The question that everybody's asked me about is: When do you think the boy band phenomenon will come to an end?" asks Dick. "And I say, well, it's been going for thirty-odd years. In terms of the idolatrous worship and screaming girls, from that perspective and the fact that let's see how many T-shirts, lamp shades, lunch boxes we can sell, there's really very little difference. Whether the Backstreet Boys will still be around in eight years' time and will be making *Abbey Road* is a different matter. At this stage in their career, they've been around two or three years, it's all about teen magazines and pinups on walls. I don't think there's really that much difference. I don't see any difference between Britney Spears and Cilla Black, in terms of where they came from; Cilla was managed by the same person that managed the Beatles; was discovered hanging around the same kind of area. Same for Britney—what's the diff? The thing that's different now is there are people in international power who were Beatles fans, and everybody who has kids now knows what it's like to have their idols.

"I think it's a truism about modern culture that every time a Beatles comes along, a Rolling Stones comes along; every time a Backstreet Boys comes along, an 'N Sync comes along, Britney—Christina Aguilera, you get *Armageddon* and *Deep Impact*," Dick continues. "For some reason, the minute one idea, which is a good idea, comes along, another one is gestating in a different part of the country at the same time, quite remarkably. I've seen it happen a hundred times. And always one has the edge on the other. It's basically down to perception because all these things are terribly subjective. Are 'N Sync songs better than Backstreet Boys songs? It depends on who you ask. It's the same with the Volkswagen—the new bug is the same car as the VW Golf, it's just got a different body on it. It's exactly the same engine. It's all about what people want to possess."

The fact that there are so many boy bands right now has led to some intense competition between the groups. None of them, however, will publicly acknowledge this rivalry.

The bands will, however, disclose that they do not

like to be referred to as "boy bands." "You can see the description: There's these young guys, a band, boy band," explains Wright. "Is it a put-down? Motown back in their time, they clowned them for being boy bands, the Jackson Five, they were a boy band."

Many of the so-called boys in these groups aren't really boys at all. 'N Sync's Chris Kirkpatrick, Backstreet Boys' Kevin Richardson, and C Note's David Perez are all in their mid- to late-twenties. And while more and more of the vocalists are picking up instruments, most groups concentrate on flashy dance moves over playing live music, so they aren't even really a band at all!

Lou Pearlman, founder of Trans-Continental Records, traces the term back to Germany. "Years ago the groups that were over there were actually bands playing music. Though they might have boys in them, they were bands because they played music. A group that would dance and sing was determined to be quoted a boy band. It started back to the times of New Kids on the Block, and it also dates back to Take That. Once they had those bands, because they didn't play instruments per se, they called them boy bands, like boy toys. So they're referring to a combination of boy toy, and they're a band, so they made it boy band."

As far as why today's bands frown upon the term, Pearlman explains, "To me, they like to say, 'No, we're a vocal group.' And I don't know why. If they were guys and they were called a girl band, I could see why they'd be upset, but certainly to call them a boy band, I don't think anybody should take it out of context. They kind of look at that and frown upon that, some of the media and press saying that that means they are not talented, can only sing and dance, and they can't play instruments. What's wrong with the fact that you can't play an instrument, but you can sing and dance? There's a lot of people out there who just sing and dance. Certainly I think that it should not be looked upon negatively. I actually think that we are a vocal group first and foremost, this is about the sound, you don't get to see the band on the radio first, you get to hear them. So if they sound good, and they look good after you see the magazines, call them whatever you want. Bottom line is, if Backstreet Boys are your favorite act, great."

No one can predict the future. How long the current trend will last is anyone's guess. Will these bands grow and evolve with their fans? Will they be able to maintain the pressures of working as a group or will each spawn a successful solo act in a few years? Rather than trying to forecast what is yet to come, let's just enjoy them while we've got them! Let's hear it for the boys!

Joey McIntyre

There is life after boy bands. That's the good news for Nick Carter, Justin Timberlake, and anyone else who might be wondering how long they can go on with their flashy dance moves, singing bubble-gum pop. All of the Beatles had successful solo careers later in life. The Jackson Five spawned Michael Jackson, the king of pop. Consider the success of New Edition's Bobby Brown,

Take That's Robbie Williams, Menudo's Ricky Martin, and most recently, New Kids on the Block's Joey McIntyre.

Graduating from a successful teen pop act does not guarantee a prosperous solo career. "Being a New Kid is great, and people love it. And being a New Kid can be a hindrance, too," admits Joey McIntyre. Sometimes it's necessary to work twice as hard to get people to accept you in a new light. For this former New Kid, being a part of pop history is something he wouldn't trade for the world. He fondly remembers the height of his experience in one of the most popular boy bands ever.

"We were still in *Hangin' Tough*, we were probably on our sixth or seventh single," recalls Joey. "We were performing in arenas across America. It was a Christmas show. We had a Christmas album out. And we were still in it together. Everyone was still doing the dance steps and it was a team. I remember that time as a great period."

Not too long after that, things began to change. "It was when we lost that loving feeling," Joey continues. "I guess it was the American Music Awards of 1990. It was an exciting night. The first award of the night was album of the year and we got it. That was pretty high, if you want to take one moment, but it wasn't a team. All of a sudden Donnie [Wahlberg] was trying to be the leader and say the perfect thing and be the great defender, so he's in his mood, and Jordan [Knight]'s doing his thing. I just wanted to go, 'Guys, wait a minute, let's have some fun.' And it pissed me off because I was only seventeen. I was the baby of the group, and I guess I have a feeling that if it was today I'd have more of a say to shake them and say, 'Listen man, let's enjoy this.' But it was as if we were fighting this war. After that it just turned into something else. We just kind of went our separate ways. It was not like it was."

After a few years out of the limelight, Joey returned to his first love—music. He had spent a couple years writing his own songs and collaborating with fellow New Kids Danny Wood and Donnie Wahlberg. "Those guys were there," says Joey. "They had the experience in the studio that I didn't have. They had the wherewithal to do what I wanted to do so it was the perfect way to start the album. We're still out there and we're still together and it is kind of romantic in a way."

Danny, who had worked on LFO's album, actually introduced Joey to Lou Pearlman. "He was like, 'You gotta meet this guy, he's got a [lot] of money and he'll make you sell a lot of albums,' " Joey recounts. In addition, Johnny Wright, who had previously operated as a tour manager for the New Kids all those years ago, was now working closely with Pearlman, managing several of his acts.

"I've known Johnny all my life, since I was twelve years old," says Joey. "But it was a different thing. It had been four years since I'd even seen him or worked with him since he'd been in Europe with the Backstreet Boys and no one really knew, but it was this thing that was kind of like New Kids, but they're getting really popular and what not. Johnny Wright had some steam and had connections over there with Lou Pearlman and I was like all right, let's do it. But I was producing it myself, so I didn't sign any contracts with anyone, with Lou or Johnny."

Over the next two years Joey continued to work on his music. "I was moving it along, I was the executive producer, I was paying for it, the whole nine yards," he explains. "We kept on talking with Lou but it never really clicked because he likes to do things his way, and I guess I thought I really had to do it on my own. So I didn't want to say, all right make me a star again. Bring me over to Europe and I'll do the boy band thing again and do all the right pictures and the magazines and be a teen idol again. I didn't want to do that. I know he had all the right connections but it just didn't feel right."

At the last minute, Joey pulled out. In March of 1998 he started going to record companies to pitch his solo album. "I'm going in there with my tail between my legs, talking to these people," Joey recalls. "They really just wanted to have lunch with an ex-New Kid and see what he's up to. They were not really interested in me. Or maybe they just didn't get the music, and didn't understand it, and here I am writing my own music for the first time, and I don't really have a track record in that area."

Head hung low, Joey returned home somewhat disappointed that no one signed him to a record deal right away. But he didn't let that stop him. "I went to the local radio station, KISS 108 [in Boston]. I played 'Stay the Same' to [music director] Kid David because it felt like a song that showed where I was coming from. I needed to learn how to love myself. I needed to believe in myself if I was gonna do this. I played it for David and he said, 'I'll play it today.'"

Although it took a few years to get the deal on his solo album, many people thought Joey waited until the height of the boy band resurgence because the timing was perfect. "Not at all," he protests. "That's unfortunate and aggravating because I don't live my life according to people's tastes. You can say it's good timing, but you can say it might have hurt me too. My life is about my music, what I do with my music. I toured all this year. I was able to perform with a great band. It's been an incredible success. Did I sell Ricky Martin numbers? No. But that doesn't bother me. You can say it's good timing, but maybe it would have been better if it wasn't the case."

Soon after Joey's success, fellow former New Kid, Jordan Knight followed suit, taking a page right out of Joey's book, going directly to radio himself. "I think I had a direct impact with how Jordan went about it," claims Joey.

"You make good music. If I get a 'Stay the Same' on each album, then I'll be fine," says Joey. "That's all I got to do. Make good music and the rest will come. We love to have everything right now. It would have been great if this was the best comeback of all time, right now. But it's even better. I know that because of New Kids, there's no where to go but up, for me. But I know I love to do what I do and that's what brings me home—just making music and being on stage and I know I love doing that and I know I'm great doing that and I want people to know that."

As for a New Kid reunion, Joey advises, "Never say never, but it's so complicated. Not only musically, but personally. Everybody's on a different page, but I think there's definitely a possibility. Jermaine Jackson is talking about how they're working on stuff and how they're getting back together. Of course I didn't say, is Michael gonna be there because that's a missing link. The Jacksons can get together forever, but if Michael isn't there, it's not a reunion. That would be cool. We could open for them, that would be a [great] tour. You never know. I still think personally we've got some [stuff] to prove. We just have to get some things over and hopefully if it happens, it happens, and we're not too old to get together."

Web Site

www.joeymcintyre.com

Elements of a Boy Band

What makes a band successful? Is it the group that has the cutest guys? Is it the singers with the freshest sound? How important is it for the artists to actually be playing instruments? Should the effort of the boys be focused on coordinated dance moves? Musicians who write their own songs have an invaluable talent, but is this a necessity to survive in the competitive world of teen music? Can fan support make or break today's top acts? Do self-collaborations merit more credit than manufactured ensembles? This chapter examines all the ingredients that are key to today's top boy bands.

Lou Pearlman, founder of Trans-Continental Records, who created the Backstreet Boys, 'N Sync, LFO, and several other top teen groups, has a list of qualities he looks for in a musical act. "One is dedication. Second is great vocal ability that can be cultivated," notes Pearlman. "Great dancing ability. If they can play instruments, that's another plus. And most importantly, is there charisma? With charisma I mean the look, and how the ladies like them. If it's a girl group, how the guys like them. How they all blend together, their harmonic sound, can they sing sweet harmonies, and so on. That's what you look for."

"Bow Legged" Lou George, a member of Full Force, the writing/producing team behind several of today's top teen songs, thinks there's nothing more important than the music. "I go to a Backstreet Boys concert, an 'N Sync concert, and you see these kids singing everything word for word," says George. "You can't fool these kids. No matter how cute a person looks, the song has still gotta be catchy to them."

Songwriter Gary Baker, who has written for everyone from Boyzone to 98 Degrees, agrees that it is the value of the song and how well it is written that are most significant. "When the melody and a lyric gel perfectly, I can't explain it . . . it's just magic," says Baker.

A song that isn't heard cannot find success. The medium that brings music to the masses is an integral part of the equation. "You can never, never downplay the importance of radio play because that's where people hear it," suggests Nigel Dick, director of such music videos as Backstreet Boys' "All I Have To Give" and Britney Spears's "Baby One More Time." "They hear it on the radio, they love it, they go and they buy it."

With the advent of MTV and the music video, a great deal of emphasis has shifted to a group's visual image. "Take the Ed Sullivan days, multiply that by ten. Make one piece, very heavily produced, create any image you want, and have it played fifty billion times," suggests deejay JoJo Wright of KIIS-FM, Los Angeles. "If the image is not there, it makes it a little more difficult. Every group has to have a personality."

A great deal of planning goes into carefully creating the image for each band. "If you look at the early videos, [the Backstreet Boys] were dressed pretty plain and simple," notes director Lionel C. Martin, who shot several music videos with the group, including "I'll Never Break Your Heart," "Anywhere For You," and "We've Got It Goin' On." "It almost looks like the clothes were grabbed straight out of the Gap. That's a good thing because it had a very natural feel and I think the kids who are looking at this stuff say, 'Hey, I like this guy . . . he looks good but he dresses like me. He doesn't look like he's that far away that I can't touch or I can't reach him.' But from a director's point of view, I want to make this group look really hot—to the girls, sexy; to the guys, have a little bit of edge to them.

"If you look at these groups, sometimes they all kind of look alike, so the clothing is critical," continues Martin. "You don't want to dress them up so far-fetched so they lose that identification factor with their audience, the people that are buying their records. But you have to make them stand out from the rest of the groups that are out there."

One of the requirements Trans-Continental places upon its artists is that they must adhere to a clean-cut, wholesome look. As such, it frowns upon piercings, facial hair, and anything that veers away from the norm, that makes one look edgy. "As [the Backstreet Boys] began to break away from Papa Lou [Martin's nickname for Pearlman], they started to get a little more spiky and outrageous in their hairstyles, facial hair: beards, mustaches, and it's just a natural part of them growing up too," notes Martin. "If you watch and compare the old to the new, they start to get a lot more into the jewelry, like the earrings and the chains. All artists across the board, I've noticed, will start to do that because as they start to get more successful, they want to show off their wealth a little bit."

Dick agrees that image is enormously consequential. "The Beatles wouldn't have been as successful without the mop-top haircuts. Britney wouldn't be as successful without the little-school-girl thing. I think it's terribly, terribly important," says Dick.

"If you're going to be hiding behind instruments, so to speak, then you don't have to worry too much about the look," advises Pearlman. "But if you're out there in front, girls always want a good-looking singer. Guys want a guy they can look up to as a class-president type. You want somebody that has a charisma."

While the ability to play music doesn't seem to be a requirement to spawn a successful group, more acts are beginning to play instruments. Whether it's a reaction to criticism that these vocal groups don't play their own songs, or simply a natural progression to begin writing and playing music, it certainly is an increasing trend. Some bands, such as Hanson, the Moffatts, and even the Beatles, chose playing live over dancing at all. Others wouldn't be able to continue their successful stage shows if they were bogged down with musical equipment.

Traditionally, dancing has been a key ingredient in

the success of teen acts. This trend was widely popularized by New Kids on the Block, but it started as early as the Jackson Five. "There's nothing like that feeling when everybody's on the same page," says former New Kid Joey McIntyre. "It's amazing. It's like the '86 Celtics. It's championship [stuff] when everybody's on the same page. But when it's not, it ain't pretty."

And of course, all elements come together most effectively in a well-produced music video. "I think with TRL being the highest-rated show on MTV right now, everybody is tuning in every day to see what the number one is," explains Dick. "On Friday of one week, nobody knows who Britney is, and by the Thursday of the following week when it started making its way up TRL, everybody in school is talking about her. The world is split into two halfs: people who like Britney and the people who don't.

"The following Saturday morning, all you hear is the patter of feet as they all rush down to the mall to buy the record," Dick continues. "And she has a career, inside eight days. That is the power of video because they not only like the music, but they think she looks cute, or she looks sexy, or I want to be Britney . . . whichever it is. That's a power that's still a truism, if your group is on TV, on the right show, you get this huge hike in album sales the next day. It's a one hundred percent, pure marketing tool, which is what pop video is meant to be. It's a sales machine, a sales item to promote a record."

The goal of marketing the bands is to make the end user a devoted fan of the group. Boy bands are only popular as long as their fans continue to support them and buy their CDs.

"If you catch the spirit or the heart of a young girl audience, they will live and die for their favorite group," says Wright. "I think they start off as, hey, they're hot and they like their music, then they feel like they know them. They go through tough times, they turn their songs on, it takes them out of bad times, or if they have a great time. Their moms like them too. They bond with their mom on this one group. Their mom hauls them up to the concert to wait in line for six hours. It's a bonding thing. It becomes a part of their life. Kind of like me, with my dad, when we talk about Dallas Cowboy football. If me and my dad went to a football game and sat on the sideline of the Dallas Cowboy Texas stadium, it would be almost a spiritual thing because it's so intense."

Fans do become loyal to their band. Wright makes an interesting observation about his listeners. "There is a rule I've noticed. I call it the 'N Sync/Backstreet Boys rule, just to get a little riot out of people sometimes. There are three main young guy groups right now: 'N Sync, Backstreet Boys, and 98 Degrees. For some unknown reason 'N Sync fans don't like the Backstreet Boys, Backstreet Boys fans don't like 'N Sync. But they can each like 98 Degrees as long as they like them to a lesser level than their favorite group. People call up and say, 'JoJo, there's not a rule.' No, there's not a rule—it's just something I've noticed."

But the big question remains, who will have lasting power and who will be a one-hit wonder? "They're gonna have to evolve, of course," says Robin Jones, program director for Radio Disney. "They're not gonna be able to be ten years from now and targeting the younger target demo. They'll have to grow with their audience."

"I think that they should take advantage of this fad, but their longevity will come out if they grow musically and if their image grows as far as baby band to the next step to the next step," suggests Wright. "Longevity is a tough game."

"When New Kids on the Block and Menudo were out, there weren't a lot of spin-off groups," says Martin. "You can probably count the number of groups that were similar. I think that's what probably is gonna kill the trend right now because every record company said I want to have a Backstreet Boys because they're making so much money.

"I think Lou also took the Menudo concept, which is when one kid got a little bit older, he replaced them with a new kid," Martin continues. "What Lou does is he tags Backstreet and he figures it has a certain life. Then he's got 'N Sync right behind. Right behind 'N Sync is LFO, which is a little bit different already. And I think that's kind of smart and I think that's what has extended this trend or sensation right now because there's a lot of people to choose from. With marketing and MTV, it's easier to keep those groups out with a little more life.

"Will we see Backstreet Boys ten years from now as Backstreet Boys? I don't think so. But what I do think will happen is probably the most talented person in any of these groups, I can see them going solo and doing a solo thing and changing up, but traditionally the teen magazine sensations are only as hot as they are until these kids grow up and then they're on VH-1's *Remember When*. Naturally, since they're so young when they start and they're so overwhelmed with all the success that sometimes these kids just want to leave and get away and be normal for a couple of years. Then sometimes they get this bug that makes them want to come back in and sometimes it's too late and sometimes they have successful comebacks.

"There's very few groups that can last all that way," says Martin. "Rolling Stones is a band that has withstood the test of time. You have to be really super talented to last that long. [It's more difficult for a group] because they start to have their differences internally with each other. I've seen discord amongst the members. If you're in a group and one member of the group becomes the one that the girls just go crazy about, I don't care what anybody says, it's got to affect the rest of the group to a certain extent."

"You can never truly predict who it's going to be," says Dick. "It's like, when you first heard 'Roxanne' did you know that Sting was going to be such a great songwriter? It's always the one you're not kind of expecting, I think."

If you want to be up there onstage in a boy band or girl group, or if you think you have what it takes to work your magic behind the scenes as a songwriter, musician, producer, or manager, harbor the passion and follow your dreams. You can make it happen if you keep your goals in sight.

"People think that this is a very simple business," says Edgardo Diaz, founder of Menudo. "If you want to be a doctor, you have to study and pass a lot of tests and work really hard. And after you get your diploma, you have to keep studying. That's the way it is. If you want to be a lawyer, it's the same thing. Almost all careers are like that. If you want to be successful, prepare yourself, study, work hard. That's the whole point."

Songwriter Gary Baker advises, "Make sure that your heart is in it and that you're willing to sacrifice whatever it takes to do it and to never give up. If you believe in yourself, don't give up, don't quit, and learn to take criticism constructively—make a positive out of it, not just a negative out of it."

Full Force's George gives his two cents on the subject. "I say just study hard, sing great, and get together with some good people behind the scenes because you could always present something to somebody, to Trans-Con or just try to present it to a record company with a good demo tape, or video, or just go to a record company and just sing a capella in front of the president. Crazy stuff like that. There's a lot of things you can do if you think it through and think right. Sometimes you don't have to go the regular way, you can come around a different way. If you're truly hungry, and truly really feel you can make it, you can just go ahead and do it."

"If God has been fortunate to give you good vocal cords, and you want to be a singer, or if you want to play instruments and you can learn quickly and catch it, my advice to them is if you can dream it, you can do it," says Pearlman. "If you can dream, reach for the stars, because it can happen. Stay at it, keep working at it, keep practicing because practice makes perfect and that's true. It never is perfect because you always want to keep learning every day, but you got to keep going."

Backstreet Boys

Several years ago five young boys formed a vocal group in Orlando, Florida. Their lives were about to change in a way none of them could ever have dreamed. None of them could possibly have imagined the impact they would have on the changing face of the music business. Since the release of their debut album in 1997, the quintet has literally redefined pop music. Firmly planted in the *Billboard* album chart's Top Twenty for close to two years, they've obtained an impressive collection of gold and platinum albums and singles, and earned an inspiring list of prestigious music industry nominations and awards. Nick Carter, Howie Dorough, Brian Littrell, AJ McLean, and Kevin Richardson, collectively known to millions of adoring fans as the Backstreet Boys, are seriously larger than life.

Nick, Howie, and AJ first met at various acting auditions in Orlando. The three became friends and started singing together. Eventually the trio resolved to fill out their sound by adding two additional members to the group who would widen their range of vocal harmonies. Through a mutual friend, the guys were introduced to Kevin, who was performing nearby at Disney World. Kevin drafted his cousin Brian, who uprooted from Kentucky to complete the group. While performing at a talent show in Orlando, they were discovered by Lou Pearlman, head of Trans-Continental Records, and the rest is history.

"A lot of people want to discount us. Because unlike a rock band or a garage band, they don't think we paid our dues," Kevin told *Rolling Stone*. "A lot of people don't know we've been together seven years. We weren't playing bars, but we played high schools all over the United States. High schools aren't bars, but teenagers are tough crowds, man."

As you can see, the boys weren't always at the top of the game. "When I started doing Backstreet Boys, nobody knew who they were," says Nigel Dick, who directed the group's music videos for "All I Have to Give" and "As Long As You Love Me."

Even after initial success in Europe, the guys themselves wanted nothing more than to find recognition in their homeland. "It was weird, because we'd play shows to, like, 10,000 fans in Europe, then we'd come back home and walk down the street and no one would recognize us," Nick told the *Los Angeles Times*. "It was a humbling experience, because now we want to show everybody, 'Look, this is what we've been doing.' "

"People think we're from London or someplace," Brian told *Entertainment Weekly* back in 1997. "But now it's time to come home. It's important to us to be recognized here."

"I'll never forget Brian telling me, 'All this European success is great, man, but it's not gonna be nothing until we can be big here at home,'" recalls "Bow Legged" Lou George, leader of the R&B writing/producing team Full Force. "They wanted so bad to be popular here in the United States, I mean *so* bad."

Today Full Force specializes in teen music, working with every youth act from LFO to Britney Spears. But it was the Backstreet Boys that helped them reinvent their own career. After producing a slew of hit records in the eighties with Jive Records artists such as Lisa Lisa and the Cult Jam, and Samantha Fox, and having had success on the silver screen with memorable roles in the *House Party* movies, business began to slow down for the family operation. That's when Barry Weiss, president and general manager of Jive Records, showed them a tape of the Backstreet Boys. "I'll never forget that meeting," says George. "He told me how he felt with the right songs they could be huge in the United States.

"We got that tape and studied it," explains George. This resulted in the song, "All I Have To Give." Although the six relatives that compose the team collectively take credit on everything they do as Full Force, it was George's cousin, Baby Gerry, who came up with the idea. "I'll never forget when he sang it to me," recalls George. "I got up and I hugged him. I said, 'Gerry, this is a smash. They're gonna love this.' As soon as we took it into Jive Records, they went crazy for it. The owner, Clive Calder, went ballistic."

Next the song was presented to the band. "Clive Calder and Barry Weiss took it into the group and the group went crazy. They loved it," says George. Although he wasn't privy to the exchange, legend has it that the guys played a joke on some of the other executives at Jive. According to George, "Clive said to them, in front of the guys, 'I don't know why you guys are excited about this Full Force song because the guys think it's [awful].' Then Nick said, 'Yeah, I don't like it, man. You guys got good ears?' Then Brian said, 'No, we don't like it.' Then they all laughed and said, 'No, we love it, we love it.' "

The instructions given to Full Force were for Nick to sing lead on the whole song. "They said Nick Carter because he was the most popular of the group, and all the girls loved him," remembers George. "Clive was going, 'Oh, my goodness, every time his face comes on the screen the girls go crazy for him.' He said that was the orders for us to do, make Nick sing the whole song and then maybe have Brian and AJ do some ad-libbing."

At this point the writing/producing team still hadn't met the boys. "The first time we met them they were great," George concedes. "Kevin Richardson knew of us mostly, because he's the oldest. The rest of the guys knew of Full Force through the movie *House Party*."

New York–based Full Force flew to Orlando to record the song. That's when George had an idea. "We heard a lot of their songs and Brian, Nick, and AJ were singing most of them, so I said, 'Let's have each one of them do a part.'

"I never used to hear anything much said about

Howie Dorough and his singing so I said we're gonna let Howie get a chance at this and if he does well, then we stick to the plan. If he sucks, then we go to [Jive's] plan," says George. "We're always down for the under-dog. We looked at Howie as the underdog in that group once we started learning 'cause nobody used to talk about him that much within the ranks. We even talked to some of the other producers and they were saying, no, this is who you should get to sing it. I mean, they're all gifted, so what we did was we tried Howie on it and he was great."

"We all came from solo backgrounds and it was just a matter of timing for us to all get our individual spot-light time," says Howie D., rumored to be the "nicest guy" in the group. "We were patient enough to take the backseat for a while, but then within time you just step up to the plate."

When you watch the video for "All I Have To Give," you'll see that the entire group is singing lead. "That's the first time they ever had something like that done in the group," says George. "I think our song was the cata-lyst for what's happening now. When their new songs come out, everybody is singing parts. It's not like back in the old days where Brian sang everything. I look at our song as the one that jump-started it."

Since they began, the Backstreet Boys have not only grown into adulthood, but they've also matured as artists. "As an artist I've become very open-minded," admits Howie. "I learned to definitely be a team player. We've really learned to be considerate of each other's feelings and each other's talents. That's one of the keys to keep a group together and successful. It's not an 'I' thing, it's a 'we' thing."

"I don't think anybody realizes exactly how difficult it can be because essentially what you've done is you've married four other people," suggests Dick. "If you look at any member of the Rolling Stones, I think you'll find that their membership in the Rolling Stones has lasted longer than probably any of their individual marriages.

"I may have done a day with the Backstreet Boys where one of them was not having a good day," Dick continues. "Well, I'm sure if you went to an office today and you picked any five people and then you worked with them for a week, you'd have a day where one of them wasn't talking to one of the others. It's inevitable."

"Communication is the best way of keeping any group together," Howie suggests. "Fighting sometimes is positive as long as you're airing out your feelings, that nobody holds stuff back from each other. Know that there's always room for improvement and always room for each other to shine and everybody can get out of it what they want."

As they continue to revolutionize the music industry, the boys take on an increasing amount of responsibility. "It's show business," says Howie. "There's a lot more to it than just performing up on stage. There's a lot of things I've learned from it."

Whether it's their heartthrob looks, their energetic performances, their talent as writers and musicians, or the way they shine on the dance floor, when it comes right down to it, it's still about the songs. "I think Backstreet Boys have had some great stuff," notes deejay

JoJo Wright, the resident guru on the teen music scene on KIIS-FM in Los Angeles. "[*Millennium*] was a great follow up to their last album. They didn't try to be something they weren't. They didn't try to get way artistic and save the world, they just did what they do. 'I Want It That Way' is a nice simple song, and that song got so many calls and so many requests and it never burned out. It has a life span of very few songs I've seen."

"I think that's what's made the Backstreet Boys so successful," agrees Gary Baker, who has written several songs for the group including "Anywhere For You," "If I Don't Have You," and "No One Else Comes Close." "Their songs are really strong. There are no fillers on a Backstreet Boys album. You could actually pick twelve singles on the *Millennium* album if you wanted."

The guys have also grown as writers. "Back to Your Heart" is a song written by Baker and Kevin Richardson. "Kevin came to my house and before he even set his stuff down, he saw my grand piano over to the right," recalls Baker. "He walked over to it and sat down and played that exact intro that you hear. He just sat there and played that, and I said, 'Wow, let's take that somewhere.'"

Baker called another writer he knew, Jason Bloom, and invited him to collaborate on the tune. "He drove down in two hours, and he liked the music we had, and we sat there and he wrote the bulk of the lyrics, and the three of us sat there and finished it. In a day's time we had that song. That was a very well-collaborated song because Kevin came in with the intro, we wrote the music, and then the three of us wrote the lyrics."

"We're touching people's lives and making people forget about their problems for a moment," Kevin told *Teen People*. "That's what music's all about, I think."

Kevin stayed at Baker's home while they worked. As you can imagine, Baker's entire family was thrilled to have a Backstreet Boy as their very own houseguest. "When Kevin was here this past summer, he would swim out in the back, and you could see all the shades tilting down: my wife and all of her friends just checking him out," laughs Baker.

Kevin and the boys are used to being checked out practically everywhere they go. It sometimes makes it virtually impossible for them to lead normal lives. "I went to a restaurant one day in Alabama with one of the guys, and we had to have a police escort to get out," Baker recalls. "That always was funny to me. By the time we got done eating, there were a hundred girls with cameras outside, and that was even before they got real big. When they come to my house now, no one knows."

"It's been unbelievable. My life has totally changed," concurs Howie, who has no regrets about the path he has chosen. "I knew there would be some sacrifices, but they're sacrifices I don't mind making. The benefits and the rewards totally outweigh the sacrifices."

The Backstreet Boys have reached a level of international super stardom that parallels that of the Beatles. In addition to their own mega-success, they've inspired a barrage of other boy bands. If *Millennium* is any indication of what's to come, we can rest assured that the boys are not a fad, and indeed are here to stay.

"The Beatles started this," AJ told *Rolling Stone*.

"They were actually the first boy band, and then, nowadays, in this whole nineties genre, it was us. We . . . put our foot in the door and then walked right through it. We became leaders. . . . As long as we stay one step ahead, and we stay leaders, hopefully we will always be on top."

"If we can grow with our fans, I think we can be around for a long time," says Howie. "As long as people are loving us and our music, and we're still loving it, I think we can be around as long as the Eagles, and the Rolling Stones."

Discography

Albums

Backstreet's Back (Europe) (Jive)
1. Everybody (Backstreet's Back)
2. As Long As You Love Me
3. All I Have To Give
4. That's The Way I Like It
5. 10,000 Promises
6. Like A Child
7. Hey Mr DJ (Keep Playin' This Song)
8. Set Adrift On Memory Bliss
9. That's What She Said
10. If You Want It To Be Good Girl
11. If I Don't Have You

Backstreet Boys (Jive)
1. We've Got It Goin' On
2. Quit Playing Games (With My Heart)

3. As Long As You Love Me
4. Everybody (Backstreet's Back)
5. All I Have to Give
6. Anywhere for You
7. Hey, Mr. DJ (Keep Playin' This Song)
8. I'll Never Break Your Heart
9. Darlin'
10. Get Down (You're the One for Me)
11. If You Want It To Be Good Girl (Get Yourself A Bad Boy)

Millennium (Jive)

1. Larger Than Life
2. I Want It That Way
3. Show Me The Meaning Of Being Lonely
4. It's Gotta Be You
5. I Need You Tonight
6. Don't Want You Back
7. Don't Wanna Lose You Now
8. The One
9. Back To Your Heart
10. Spanish Eyes
11. No One Else Comes Close
12. The Perfect Fan

Singles

We've Got It Goin' On

Everybody (Backstreet's Back)

As Long As You Love Me

I'll Never Break Your Heart

Quit Playing Games (With My Heart)

All I Have To Give

I Want It That Way

Larger Than Life

Show Me The Meaning Of Being Lonely

Compilations

Hit Mix 97 (ZYX Records)
Quit Playing Games (With My Heart)—Backstreet Boys

Booty Call (Jive)
If You Stay—Backstreet Boys

Casper: A Spirited Beginning (EMD/Capitol)
I Wanna Be With You—Backstreet Boys

MTV Party To Go '98 (Tommy Boy)
Quit Playing Games (With My Heart)—Backstreet Boys

Hit Mix 98 (ZYX)
Everybody (Backstreet's Back)—Backstreet Boys

110% Hits (Beast)
We've Got It Goin' On—Backstreet Boys (CL's Anthem
   Radio mix)

Club Mix '98: Volume 2 (Cold Front)
As Long As You Love Me—Backstreet Boys

Jive Dance Party Hits (Jive)
As Long As You Love Me—Backstreet Boys (Soul Solution mix)

Jock Jams Volume 4 (Tommy Boy)
Everybody (Backstreet's Back)—Backstreet Boys

Sabrina, The Teenage Witch (Universal/Geffen)
Hey, Mr. DJ (Keep Playin' This Song)—Backstreet Boys (radio mix)

Club Mix '99 (Cold Front)
Everybody (Backstreet's Back)—Backstreet Boys

Ultimate Dance Party 1999 (Arista Records)
Everybody (Backstreet's Back)—Backstreet Boys

MTV Party To Go '99 (Tommy Boy)
As Long As You Love Me—Backstreet Boys

Pepsi World: The Album (Damian Music)
Quit Playing Games (With My Heart)—Backstreet Boys (Jazzy Jim's Slamma)

1999 Grammy Nominees—Mainstream (Elektra)
Everybody (Backstreet's Back)—Backstreet Boys

Boom! Vol. 2 (Beast)
All I Have To Give—Backstreet Boys

Jock Jams Vol. 5 (Tommy Boy)
All I Have To Give—Backstreet Boys (remix)

YM Hot Tracks Vol. 1 [ECD] (Damian Music)
As Long As You Love Me—Backstreet Boys

Drive Me Crazy (Jive)
I Want It That Way—Backstreet Boys (Jack D. Elliot remix)

Web Sites

www.backstreetboys.com

www.peeps.com/bsboys

Fan Clubs

Backstreet Boys
c/o Jive Records
137-139 West 25th Street
New York, New York 10001

Backstreet Boys Fan Club
P.O. Box 695004
Orlando, Florida 32869-5004

You can also write to the UK fan club:

Backstreet Boys Fan Club
P.O. Box 20
Manchester M60 3ED
U.K.

BBMak

Sitting in the upscale café at the Mondrian Hotel located on Hollywood's famous Sunset Strip, BBMak talk about their humble beginnings while devouring a healthy breakfast. The Mondrian is home to the guys' favorite hot spot—the Sky Bar, the trendiest club in LA, where if you're not on the list, you don't get in. Luckily, the guys rate admittance and can be found among the ranks of Quincy Jones, Elizabeth Hurley, Matt Dillon, and Alfonso Ribiero ("Carlton on *The Fresh Prince*. It was the only time I've been starstruck," admits Christian Burns, who is the band's oldest member).

Before the guys found glitz and glamour, they were back in their hometown of London, England, playing any pub that would have them. "We were all in different bands at the time and we were doing gigs in England. We used to bump into each other over and over," says Mark Barry, a handsome-leading-man type. "After a period of about six months of knowing each other, we decided that we recognized each other's qualities and we started to form BBMak and take it more seriously."

The band's name stems from the first letters of the guy's last names: *B*urns, *B*arry, and Ste *Mc*Nally, the group's sexy, shy, third and final member. Once the boys started playing together, they knew they were in for something big. "We complement each other vocally," says Ste, which is short for Stephen. "We've sung together for four years and we sound like one voice."

Don't expect this boy band to dance, they're too busy playing instruments when they perform live onstage. And offstage, when they're not rehearsing, they keep busy writing new songs. "There's no rules as a songwriter," says Mark.

"The inspiration is to write a great song, regardless of what it's about," says Christian. "We try and keep the melodies really strong so if it stands up as a great song just on an acoustic guitar, it's gonna get even better when we get production on it."

"We've all got the ability to write great songs on our own," adds Ste. "We don't have to work as a team to write a great song, but we get an even better song when we do work together."

Working together led them to a deal with Disney's Hollywood Records. Being part of the Disney team is no Mickey Mouse operation. In fact, it has provided BBMak with great opportunities.

If the boys could be any Disney character, Ste would be Mickey Mouse because "his girlfriend is cute." "I'd be Donald Duck," says Christian, "because I'm quite hyperactive and I get in trouble a lot." Mark would be Goofy because he playfully jokes that he's a dog.

Being in the limelight certainly has its moments, but it's not all fun and games. Just ask Christian about his stalker. "I had this girl who used to follow me around, and one day she found out where I lived and she turned up at me house," he recounts. "She got me phone number off this piece of paper in the backseat of me car, and phoned up the house pretending to be British Telecom, asking, 'Can we send some free information out? We just need to check your address.' So she found the address and came around to stalk, sending me handcuffs and blow-up dolls and other strange stuff."

Of course Christian has done a bit of stalking himself. "I got the police to track somebody down," admits the former altar boy. "Me friend's a police officer, and I got to get somebody's address." That somebody was a girl, of course, who had caught his eye. He called her up and went out on a date.

I'm sure any girl would be thrilled to have this British babe tracking her down. But if he finds you, be aware of some bizarre behavior. "I sleepwalked out the door of me mom's house naked when I was fifteen," recalls Christian. "I woke up trying to get into the car. It was four o'clock in the morning. I've done it about three times since."

And think twice before hitching a ride with Ste. "When we signed our record deal, we went on holiday to Cyprus together. I was riding a scooter and heading down to the beach. There was a bar full of people, and I drove into the sand and lost control of the bike. I hit a post. I didn't injure myself, just fell off the bike. The bar full of people just stood around laughing."

"Including me and Mark," adds wiseguy Christian.

For fans who want to get involved with the music business, BBMak offers this advice. "Follow your heart," says Christian. "Don't give up. If anyone tells you anything otherwise, ignore it."

"Be positive," offers Mark.

"Believe in yourself," adds Ste.

"Get the positives, screw them in your head. Take the negatives, and stomp them till they're dead." This motto worked for Christian, and as BBMak continues to flourish, they'll never have to look back.

Discography

Album

Sooner Or Later (Telstar)

1. Back Here
2. Still On Your Side
3. Next Time
4. I Can Tell
5. Again
6. Can't Say
7. Miss You More
8. Emily's Song
9. September
10. Sooner Or Later
11. More Than Words

Single

Back Here

Web Site

www.bbmak.co.uk

Fan Clubs

BBMak
c/o Hollywood Records
170 Fifth Avenue, Ninth Floor
New York, New York 10010-5911

BBMak
c/o Hollywood Records
500 South Buena Vista
Burbank, California 91521

Boyzone

They're probably the biggest boy band ever to come out of Ireland, but Boyzone might want to rethink their name. After sixteen UK hit singles including six number-one songs, the boys are starting to look a little rough around the edges. Perhaps these young Dubliners should be dubbed a grown-up man band.

"They've already got themselves across as men, whereas Five [their main UK competition] are still seen as boys," noted Liz Laskowski, London-based director of programming for music video channel the Box, to *Billboard*.

The Irish vocal group consists of Keith Duffy, Stephen Gately, Mikey Graham, Ronan Keating, and Shane Lynch. To their credit, the guys have never forgotten their working-class roots or where they came from.

"We know we're lucky," Ronan tells the *Examiner*. "We have never forgotten that we could still be fixing cars or taking exams or just dreaming of what will never now be. We got in at the perfect time."

Fame hasn't changed them a bit. "Once we come off-stage and unwind, we're back to the same guys we've always been," adds Keith, according to the *San Francisco Chronicle*.

Boyzone were discovered when the members answered an ad placed by Dublin nightclub owner Louis Walsh, looking for good-looking young male singers. These lucky lads were selected from a group of more than three hundred hopefuls. "It's every guy's dream to be in a band," Ronan told *USA Today*. "We're no different."

The band initially began covering songs by other pop boy bands such as the Osmonds and the BeeGees. Walsh's initial intention in putting the band together was to emulate the success of the then freshly split British guy group Take That. He even went so far as to recruit Ray Hedges, the primary songwriter for the legendary band, to collaborate with the boys on some songs.

It's clearly no surprise that like Take That, Boyzone's music ranges from up-tempo, hi-NRG dance tunes to beautiful R&B ballads. "I think it's our melodies that are the primary appeal," Ronan, a onetime shoe sales-man, told the *San Francisco Chronicle*. "Our albums have been very melodic, very radio-friendly. They're songs that, once you hear them, you can't get them out of your head."

"The Spice Girls opened the doors for a lot of artists," Stephen told the *San Francisco Chronicle*. "I think people want to hear happy pop music again, so we hope to come in on that. There's always been pop boy bands, but the way it has been in the business is, certain years it's a really strong trend and certain years it's not."

Stephen recently made international headlines when he followed another trend, that of being a high-profile celebrity coming out of the closet. "This is the hardest thing I have ever had to do," Stephen told the *London Sun*. "But I owe it to our fans as well as myself to be completely honest.

"I desperately wanted to be a pop star but decided early on I couldn't do that and be gay. I had to keep it to myself. Being honest would mean saying goodbye to fame," he noted to the *Sunday Times Magazine*. "Knowing that [the band] understood and supported me helped me with the pressure that was building up."

Both the fans and the band have stood by openly gay Stephen. "I could have gone either way," Ronan told *This Is London* about his bandmate Stephen's decision to publicly announce his homosexuality. "But [the fans] have backed him 100 percent, and it has increased our fan base. We have gained more fans than we've ever had, and our gay audience is bigger than ever, so it's turned out great in the end. You have to take your hat off to Stephen. It is probably one of the gutsiest moves he will ever have to make in his whole life."

Like all the guys in Boyzone, Stephen is in a healthy relationship. Since his announcement, he's been dating Dutch pop star Eloy de Jong of the defunct boy band Caught in the Act. Ronan is one of three members who is married. He also has a young son. Shane, whose sisters are Edele and Keavy from the girl group B*witched, is married to Esther Bennett of yet another band, Eternal. Keith Duffy is married as well, and Mikey Graham and his girlfriend have a daughter together.

The band members have obviously achieved success in their personal lives. And there's no doubt that this is one of the biggest bands of all time to come out of the U.K. But for some unknown reason, Boyzone has never managed to crack the U.S. market.

"It's frustrating," Ronan told *Billboard*. "Especially when you see bands that started after us having Top Ten hits, and you think, 'We were there before them.' "

"We would love to make it here [in the U.S.]," Stephen told the *San Francisco Chronicle* on a recent trip to the States. "It's very rewarding and you gain a lot of respect."

Ironically, like Take That alum Robbie Williams, Ronan is also beginning to make it in the U.S.—as a solo act. His song "When You Say Nothing At All," which he recorded for the *Notting Hill* soundtrack, gathered much critical acclaim. According to the *Examiner*, Ronan received 2.5 million British pounds for his first solo album, *Once Upon a Lifetime*. Boyzone's "No Matter What," which was also on the *Notting Hill* soundtrack, didn't really make an impression on the U.S. charts.

Ronan fever is equally strong in the U.K. In addition to his duties as a member of Boyzone and focusing on his budding solo career, he's also writing a book on his life and co-managing the Irish boy band Westlife, who knocked their manager off the charts in August 1999 to become the first boy band to have consecutive number ones with their first two singles. "I've had two weeks at number one, and I couldn't be happier to be knocked off by Westlife," Ronan told the *Examiner*.

Fans worry that Ronan's individual success will lead to the demise of the group. In fact, manager Walsh confirmed to the *Examiner* that Boyzone are to split up. The same article noted the future plans of the remaining Boyzone members: Stephen and Mike are both going solo. Shane plans to become a full-time race car driver. Keith wants to get into television.

But is an impending breakup truly on the horizon? We hope not. "We're sick and tired of reading that we're going to split up, and the fact that it's our manager who keeps putting out the stories really winds us up," Shane told the *Examiner*. "He's a complete jerk and only does it when he thinks we need help shifting concert tickets. You know, if people think it's the last Boyzone concert tour, they'll buy their tickets sooner."

A breakup at this point would be terribly disappointing. It could also squelch plans for a Boyzone movie in which U2's Bono is being considered to portray the band's manager. The film would be similar in tone to the Beatles' *A Hard Day's Night*.

"We've lasted longer than everyone expected, and we're not going to die," Ronan told *USA Today*. "We're proud of what we achieved. How much longer? Time will tell."

Discography

Albums

Said and Done (Polydor)
1. Together
2. Coming Home Now
3. Love Me For A Reason
4. Oh Carol
5. When All Is Said And Done
6. So Good
7. Can't Stop Me
8. I'll Be There
9. Key To My Life
10. If You Were Mine
11. Arms Of Mary
12. Believe In Me
13. Father And Son

Different Beat (Polydor)
1. Paradise
2. A Different Beat
3. Melting Pot
4. Ben
5. Don't Stop Looking For Love
6. Isn't It A Wonder
7. Words
8. It's Time
9. Games Of Love
10. Strong Enough
11. Heaven Knows
12. Crying In The Night

13. Give A Little
14. She Moves Through The Fair
15. What Can You Do For Me
16. Angel

Different Beat (+Bonus CD) (PolyGram)

1. Paradise
2. Different Beat
3. Melting Pot
4. Ben
5. Don't Stop Looking For Love
6. Isn't It A Wonder
7. Words
8. It's Time
9. Games Of Love
10. Strong Enough
11. Heaven Knows
12. Crying In The Night
13. Give A Little
14. She Moves Through The Fair

Where We Belong (PolyGram)

1. I'll Never Not Need You
2. Walk On (So They Told Me)
3. All The Time In The World
4. No Matter What
5. Picture Of You
6. Baby Can I Hold You
7. All That I Need
8. One Kiss At A Time
9. And I

10. That's How Love Goes
11. Where Did You Go?
12. Will Be Yours
13. Must Have Been High
14. You Flew Away
15. I Love The Way You Love Me

By Request (PolyGram)
1. I Love The Way You Love Me
2. No Matter What
3. All That I Need
4. Baby Can I Hold You Tonight
5. Picture Of You
6. Isn't It A Wonder
7. Different Beat
8. Words
9. Father And Son
10. So Good
11. Coming Home Now
12. Key To My Life
13. Love Me For A Reason
14. When The Going Gets Tough
15. You Needed Me
16. When You Say Nothing At All
17. All The Time In The World
18. I'll Never Not Need You
19. So They Told Me

Singles Box Set (Polydor)
1. Love Me For A Reason
   Daydream Believer

2. Key To My Life (Radio Edition)
   Key To My Life
   When Will You Understand
3. So Good
   Here To Eternity
   So Good (The Deadly Mix)
4. Father And Son (Live)
   Should Be Missing You Now
   Father & Son (Live)
5. Coming Home Now
   Close To You
   Coming Home Now (Steve Jervier Mix)
6. Words
   Price Of Love
   Words (Alternative Mix)
7. Different Beat (Radio Edition)
   Angel
   Different Beat (Remix)
8. Isn't It A Wonder
   Experiencia Religiosa
   Get Up & Get Over
9. Picture Of You
   Let The Message Run Free
   Words (Spanglish Version)
10. Baby Can I Hold You
    Shooting Star
    Mystical Experience
    Mystical Experience (Remix)
11. All That I Need (7 Edit)
    Never Easy
    Paradise
    Workin' My Way Back To You

12. No Matter What
    Where Have You Been
    All That I Need
13. I Love The Way You Love Me
    Waiting For You
    Let The Message Run Free
14. When The Going Gets Tough
    What A Wonderful World
    Love Can Build A Bridge
15. You Needed Me
    Words Can't Describe
    Megamix (Love To Infinity)
16. Every Day I Love You
    No Matter
    Will I Ever See You

Singles

Love Me For A Reason

Key To My Life

So Good

Father And Son

Words

Isn't It A Wonder

Picture Of You

Baby Can I Hold You

All That I Need

No Matter What

I Love The Way You Love Me

You Needed Me

Everyday I Love You

Compilations

Bean: The Album (Mercury)
Picture Of You—Boyzone

BOP BOYS (Interhit)
Love Me For A Reason (Boyzone)

Notting Hill (Soundtrack) (Island)
No Matter What—Boyzone

YM Hot Tracks Vol. 1 [ECD] (Damian Music)
Baby Can I Hold You—Boyzone

Web Sites

www.boyzone.co.uk

www.islanddefjam.com/boyzone

Fan Club

Boyzone
c/o Island Records
825 Eighth Avenue
New York, New York 10019

C Note

There couldn't be a better time for C Note to enter the music scene. After all, it's not only the height of the modern boy band renaissance, but also the explosion of Latin crossover artists like Marc Antony and Jennifer Lopez. This is all good for C Note, which is positioned by Trans-Continental Records as the newest edition of the Backstreet Boys injected with a heavy dose of Enrique Iglasias, bringing a sensual Latin flavor to a pleasant blend of pop, dance, and R&B sounds.

C Note has four members. Raul Molina, born in the Dominican Republic, is Mr. Personality. His warmth and charm shine in his conversation as well as his singing. Andrew Rogers, better known as Dru, is the group's blond surfer standout who only began singing once he discovered it was a great way to impress girls. David Perez, nicknamed D'LO, passed up a college basketball scholarship to pursue an entertainment career. With his suave Ricky Martin looks, this half-Cuban, half-Puerto Rican guy definitely gives Dru stiff competition as group hunk. Last but not least, Puerto Rican–born Jose "Brody" Martinez is the shy and quiet type, until he opens his mouth to sing and silences all around him with his beautiful voice.

These young studs know how important image is to a band like theirs, and tonight they strut their stuff down the catwalk at a Charlie Lapson Fashion Show to benefit the LA Shanti organization, which provides counseling, emotional support services, and education for people affected by HIV/AIDS and other life-threatening illnesses. Tossed in with actors and models alike, the boys of C Note hold their own and draw thunderous applause as they show off the clothes. In perfect brotherly style, the guys walk out together, supporting each other in this new venture of runway modeling.

If you've ever seen C Note in person, or even if you've only seen photos, you'll know these boys have it going on. But they're so much more than a group of pretty faces. And the audience, who came strictly for fashion, gets treated to a musical set from these boy wonders after the show that is more than worth the price of admission alone.

Songs like "Spanish Fly" and "Wait Till I Get Home," which was recorded in both English and Spanish, get everybody's toes tapping. The catchy tunes from their debut CD are easily distinguishable from the music of other boy bands.

C Note's well-polished act comes only after much hard work and preparation. "There's no higher expectations in the world that anybody could ever put on us than we do," admits Dru. "Our work ethic is insane."

Brody, Raul, and David started working together as a trio when two members of their previous vocal ensemble left the group. They asked their friend Dru to perform with them at a local talent contest where they were discovered by Trans-Continental Records.

According to Raul, it was Dru, the newest member of the group, who actually came up with the name. "We were going through a list of names and it wasn't even on the list that we had come up with. He just said it, C Note, and we all liked it. After a while we put our own thing to it: 'Create Nothing Other Than Excellence,' but mainly we liked the C Note, the 100 percent, it's got the play on words: the note *C* and the hundred-dollar bill. That's why we liked it. That's why it stuck."

Because Orlando is base camp to many musical acts, the guys often see their competition when they go out on the town. "We'll be in Orlando out at a club and you'll look over and you'll see one of the fellas and you're like, 'What's up?' " says David. "You'll go get a drink and hang out." Of course, just read the liner notes on *Different Kind of Love,* the group's first album, and you'll quickly find that the competition is very friendly as they acknowledge everyone from LFO to 'N Sync, wishing them much luck and success.

Superstardom happens quickly when you're young and cute and signed to a record deal by Lou Pearlman. The Orlando-based quartet quickly got a lesson in celebrity and the insanity that accompanies it.

"We were in a show in West Palm Beach [Southern

Florida], and I'd just eaten a blow pop," recalls Brody. "My cousin [Cesar "Ceez" Otero], who is also our stage manager, said that fans were asking for my blow-pop stem and they were bidding on it! 'Oh, I'll give you twenty bucks for it'—having a little auction for my blow-pop stem. That was pretty bizarre. I just threw it away."

Not all fan encounters are crazy. Some can be pretty special. "We were at a show in Huntsville, Alabama, and after the show we were going to get something to eat and we were looking to our right side and there were these people bobbing their heads in their car just jamming and singing along with a song," recalls Dru. "We were like, what are they listening to? So we rolled down the window. They were listening to 'Wait Till I Get Home,' our first single. It was awesome. That was the moment that we knew it was coming, it was almost here."

One of the benefits of their newfound stardom is the constant attention they receive from the opposite sex. But how do four eligible bachelors decide who gets which girl without fighting over them? "We let them decide," declares David. "And if that doesn't work, we just put the boxing gloves on and get in the ring and whoever wins gets the girl," adds Raul.

Female fans who want to catch their attention probably don't really need any help. "We don't have to advise them because they come up with some very good stuff," says Raul. "They know which way you're coming out of a building and they'll be hiding in a car. The other one will be like, 'I got him.' They'll jump in the car and they'll follow us ten miles to the hotel."

Despite some close encounters, overall it's been an

enjoyable experience that none of the guys would ever trade. "If you can't make light of what you do, you shouldn't be doing it," says Dru. "We're just four guys having a great time. We're doing what we love to do and that's all that matters."

Discography
Album
Different Kind Of Love (Epic)
1. Wait Till I Get Home
2. I Like
3. One Night With You
4. A Tear Or Two
5. Right Next To Me
6. My Heart Belongs To You
7. Love Of All Time
8. Feels So Good
9. Different Kind Of Love
10. Tell Me Where It Hurts
11. Spanish Fly—(featuring Mangu)
12. No Dejo De Pensar

Single
Wait Till I Get Home

Compilation
Music Of The Heart: The Album (Epic)
One Night With You—C Note

Web Sites

www.cnote.com

www.epicrecords.com/epiccenter/custom/1079

Fan Clubs

The C Note Official International Fan Club
P.O. Box 5128
Bellingham, Washington 98227

C Note
c/o Trans-Continental Entertainment
7380 Sand Lake Road, Suite 305
Orlando, Florida 32819

raul@cnote.com
dru@cnote.com
brody@cnote.com
david@cnote.com

5ive

Numbers have long been a favorite inclusion in generating band names. 3T, 311, 98 Degrees, 911, 10,000 Maniacs, All-4-One, Blink 182, Boyz II Men, Eifel 65, Eve 6, M2M, Sixpence None the Richer, Third Eye Blind, and Third Storee are but a few of the numbered musical entrees. But there's a new digit climbing the charts these days, and while they're on their way to number one, we've come to know them simply as 5ive.

All are talented and good-looking, so defining the members of this band rests on their unique personalities. Sweet-as-can-be Rich Neville, funny boy Scott Robinson, laid-back Abs Breen, oldest and wisest J Brown, and the mysteriously intriguing Sean Conlon make up the quintet that obviously derives its name from its head count. When asked how to properly write the band's moniker, Abs told *Teen Beat*, "How should you write it? Any way you want to, mate, you decide." Five, 5ive, or 5 are all equally acceptable.

The biggest boy band to come out of London since Take That (which of course spawned solo sensation Robbie Williams), the successful British phenom has already begun to make waves across the Atlantic. Their hit song "When the Lights Go Out," from their self-titled first album, not only debuted at number one in England but also landed in Billboard's Top Ten in the United States. They have similar high hopes for their highly anticipated follow-up album, *Invincible*.

Known in their homeland as the Spice Boys, this group of energetic performers has much in common with their now defunct girl-group counterpart. There may be a reason these two acts are the most successful pop groups to come out of England in the last couple years. Safe Management's Chris and Bob Herbert, the successful team behind the Spice Girls, also created and manage 5ive.

The late Bob Herbert, a former accountant, was a visionary not unlike a famous someone in Orlando, Florida. While Lou Pearlman was having success after success putting together bands at Trans-Continental Records, Bob and his son Chris followed Pearlman's example and started doing the same in England.

In creating 5ive, the first step was to put out the word that they were seeking five talented boys who could sing and dance, so they announced a casting call. The response was overwhelming and more than three thousand young men auditioned for the group. From there, the Herberts narrowed it down to their top twenty choices and asked the finalists to come in for a callback. While waiting in the lobby, five lads struck up a conversation and decided to pact together and audition as a group. The team conducting the auditions was so impressed by the quintet's unity that the boys were chosen and the band was officially formed.

The original lineup was Scott, J, Sean, Rich and *Rich,* but because the guys felt that having two Riches in the same group might prove somewhat confusing to fans, Rich Breen started going by Abs. The name is not derived from his tight physique, as many suspect, but rather is short for his middle name, Abidin.

Though they were virtually strangers until that fateful audition, the members of 5ive are now the closest of chums. Being in the spotlight doesn't make them immune to the perils of growing up and the challenges of getting along that all teens face. "We have our arguments," Scott admits to *Teen Beat.* "We don't try to say, 'Oh, we never argue,' because that would be false. We do argue a lot sometimes. But, we know we're friends by the end of the day. We know that we're not falling out, we'll still be friends."

"We know each other very well, but friends argue," Abs concedes to *Teen Beat.* "We don't get sick of each other, but yes, we get annoyed at each other every now and again—but so do couples. I mean, we work together, we see each other a lot of the time."

To move the bonding process along at a rapid pace, the guys shared an apartment when they first started working together. Rooming with each other paid off well, as anyone who's ever seen their live show can verify, because the chemistry onstage is so genuine and fun.

When the boys aren't writing new music, performing, or touring, civilian life isn't exactly normal. "I live a totally different life," Rich tells *Teen Beat All-Star*. "Before I was at school in a band with my friends. We didn't have any serious ambitions and I knew it; it was just fun. Now I'm traveling around the world, working every day. There's not a lot of time off, that's the down side. You do want to see your family more, and enjoy your fame and your money, and you really just don't have the time."

Most of 5ive's first album is written and produced by Max Martin and the late Denniz PoP, two industry legends who were responsible for writing many hit songs for today's top boy bands. Rich told *Billboard* that he is used to the band being compared to the Backstreet Boys and 'N Sync. "As performers, there are similarities in that we all do dance routines," he says. "But there haven't been a lot of boy groups from England, so we've got our British sense of humor. Also, 5ive's music is a little bit harder and edgier, because a lot of our songs are rap-based. We strongly believe there's room for everyone."

"The idea was to try and find some kids with a little attitude, a little more edgy, a little more street," Chris Herbert told the *New York Post*. But don't let their rough exterior fool you; these guys will make any young gal melt.

Thomas Martin, the band's spokesman at Arista Records, described the band to *USA Today:* "5ive are a little edgier and more urban hip-hop." But J clarifies to *Teen Beat All-Star*, "We're doing pop music and sometimes we put rap in it, but that's not hip-hop."

5ive definitely wants to be in the pop game, and they're proud of their rising status to that extent. "We're like the biggest pop band in Britain," J told *Teen Beat All-Star*. "So what other bands took two years to do, we did in four months."

"Other bands concentrate on one area," explains Sean to *Teen Beat All-Star*. "Backstreet Boys stayed in Germany for about a year before they came to America. We don't stay anywhere for longer than three days. We haven't left Europe just to do America. We're still doing Europe."

In fact, 5ive is doing it all and they should be around for a long time to come. "It's not like we're saying we can't wait for it to be over, but it's a well-known fact that pop groups end," admits J.

"We don't think we've gone as far as we can yet," Sean told *Teen Beat*. "We still have a long way to go yet for us." At the very least, five more years.

Discography

Albums

5ive (Arista)

1. When The Lights Go Out
2. That's What You Told Me
3. It's The Things You Do
4. When I Remember When
5. Slam Dunk (Da Funk)
6. Satisfied
7. It's All Over
8. Partyline 555-On-Line
9. Until The Time Is Through

10. Everybody Get Up
11. My Song
12. Got The Feelin'

Invincible (Arista)

1. If Ya Gettin' Down
2. Keep On Movin'
3. Don't Wanna Let You Go
4. We Will Rock You
5. Two Sides To Every Story
6. You Make Me A Better Man
7. Invincible
8. It's Alright
9. Serious
10. How Do Ya Feel
11. Everyday
12. Mr Z
13. Sunshine
14. Battlestar

Single

When The Lights Go Out

Compilations

YM Hot Tracks Vol. 1 (Damian Music)
It's The Things You Do—5ive

Sabrina, the Teenage Witch (Universal/Geffen)
Slam Dunk (Da Funk)

Web Sites

www.5ive.co.uk/index2.htm

www.aristarec.com/aristaweb/Five

www.5ive.co.ukanclub/index.htm

Fan Club

5ive
c/o Arista Records
Six West 57th Street
New York, New York 10019

Hanson

Many people don't realize it, but Hanson is the group credited with ending the drought of boy bands lasting since the early nineties when the New Kids on the Block performed their farewell concert. In fact, it was this family trio that paved the way for a whole new flock of musically inclined teen idols. So while the Backstreet Boys may be the biggest guy group in the last ten years, they never could have achieved their status if it weren't for the initial success of three brothers who hail from Tulsa, Oklahoma.

"Since we first put Hanson on a cover several months back, our circulation has increased 50 percent," Carrie Yasuda, managing editor of the monthly teen magazines *Bop* and *BB*, told the *Los Angeles Times* back in 1997.

"Hanson blew the lid off the whole thing," Hedy End, editorial director for *SuperTeen* and *Superstars* told the *Los Angeles Times*. "We're very happy about them and the groups they've opened the door for—like the Backstreet Boys, Boyzone, 98 Degrees, and No Authority."

But unlike many of the groups they paved the way for, Hanson grew organically—in other words, they were not manufactured and put together by a management team. Three brothers unmistakably identified by their long blond hair make up Hanson, although a recent change in hairstyle has caused an uproar among some fans. Guitar-playing oldest brother Isaac (but you can call him Ike) is serious and sweet, but he also has a sly sense of humor. Keyboardist Taylor sings lead vocals, but don't think this middle child suffers from Jan Brady syndrome. Tay is a favorite among female fans who notice that offstage, when this Hanson is not performing for a crowd, he's adorably shy. Youngest brother Zac is loud, hyper, and a bundle of energy, which is why he's most suited to the instrument he plays, the drums.

It's hard to believe that just five years ago the three teenage brothers were singing a cappella, without instruments, at local fairs and festivals in their hometown of Tulsa, Oklahoma. A few years went by before the boys picked up instruments and became an actual band, originally calling themselves the Hanson Brothers.

"We got the drums and the instruments and then a week later we played live," Taylor told MTV. "But that doesn't mean we were good when we played live."

Isaac, Taylor, and Zac traveled the world even before they became famous and started touring as a band. Their dad was an oil company executive and the family had to move around a lot, so the boys grew up in many exotic locations.

When they lived in South America, the guys couldn't understand the radio stations, so instead they listened incessantly to a Time/Life collection of the history of rock and roll. Their earliest musical recollections were of artists like Aretha Franklin, Chuck Berry, and the Supremes.

Isaac wrote his first song, "Rain Falling Down" when he was in the third grade. Once their dad, Walker, recognized above-average talent in his sons' musical abilities, he quit his job to oversee the group.

The boys and their four younger siblings are all home-schooled by their mother. In an interview with *US* magazine, Zac said, "Our mom wanted to home-school us because she wanted to have a better relationship with us."

Of missing out on that "normal" high school experience, Isaac told *US,* "I missed out on getting dumped by about 10 million girls. Getting beat up by bullies. Peer pressure." They also would have missed the opportunity to achieve worldwide success with their band!

If anything, the success of Hanson has made the family an even tighter unit. Zac told the *San Francisco Chronicle,* "The whole family is actually with us on the tour because we're gone for two or three months, so, you know, might as well take 'em. We've got a big enough bus."

The big breakthrough for Hanson came with the debut of *Middle of Nowhere,* which was their first album released on a major record label. When the boys were only sixteen, thirteen, and eleven years old, "MMMBop," the humable tune that was originally written as a background part for another song, took over the number one spot and propelled the teens into superstardom.

The boys took a long break after the hysteria from the first album died down. In the interim, they released a holiday-themed record and a live concert album. Last year the band returned to the recording studio to work on *This Time Around,* their highly anticipated follow-up album.

On the new album, Hanson shares the spotlight with guest artists such as John Popper of Blues Traveler and fellow teen superstar, blues-rocker Jonny Lang. "He's a better musician than all of us," Taylor told MTV of Lang. "He puts us to shame."

"The guy is an amazing guitarist," Isaac added. "It is very cool to know a guy your age who can play like that, it is really inspiring," notes Isaac on the band's official Web site.

The brothers co-produced the new album with Stephen Lironi, who also produced *Middle of Nowhere.* Incredibly, the Hansons wrote *all* the songs themselves. They clearly have continued to grow, not only as musicians and performers, but as songwriters.

One of the guys' favorite parts about being in a band is performing in front of a live audience. "I don't think anybody is ever quiet," Zac told MTV about the overwhelming audience feedback that greets the band at their concerts. "There's always a constant 'aaahhh!' "

"It's definitely cool to go out and sing for sixty thousand people and have them singing your song back at you," Taylor told the *San Francisco Chronicle*. "That's one of those things you can't describe. It truly is awesome."

Taylor also told the *Los Angeles Times,* "All these screaming girls and guys going crazy, you just have to have fun with it."

But has fame gotten to these young teen sweeties? "We kind of don't really think of ourselves as being famous," Taylor told the *Boston Globe*. "We don't. We're very, very normal."

"It is very weird to get thousands of letters and hundreds of thousands of e-mails a day from all over the world," Taylor adds.

"We just try to stay ourselves," notes Isaac.

"I would definitely say we've had to mature a little bit," Zac told the *San Francisco Chronicle*. "Because we're doing business. We have a job. This is what we do—it's not like we can goof off all the time."

Of course, as far as jobs go, being rock musicians isn't so bad. As Taylor told *US* magazine, "How much better of a job could you possibly have than to be in a band your whole life?"

Discography

Albums

Middle Of Nowhere (Mercury)

1. Thinking Of You
2. MMMBop
3. Weird

4. Speechless
5. Where's The Love
6. Yearbook
7. Look At You
8. Lucy
9. I Will Come To You
10. A Minute Without You
11. Madeline
12. With You In Your Dreams
13. Man From Milwaukee—(CD Only, Garage Mix)

Middle Of Nowhere (+Bonus Tracks) (Mercury)

1. Thinking Of You
2. MMMBop
3. Weird
4. Speechless
5. Where's The Love
6. Yearbook
7. Look At You
8. Lucy
9. I Will Come To You
10. A Minute Without You
11. Madeline
12. With You In Your Dreams
13. MMMBop
14. Man From Milwaukee

Snowed In (Mercury)

1. Silent Night Medley
2. Merry Christmas Baby
3. What Christmas Means To Me
4. Little Saint Nick

5. At Christmas
6. Christmas (Baby Please Come Home)
7. Rockin' Around The Christmas Tree
8. Christmas Time
9. Everybody Knows The Claus
10. Run Rudolph Run
11. Silent Night Medley: O Holy Night
12. Silent Night / O Come All Ye Faithful
13. White Christmas
14. O Come All Ye Faithful
15. White Christmas

Snowed In (+Bonus Tracks) (Limited Edition)
(PolyGram)

1. Merry Christmas Baby
2. What Christmas Means To Me
3. Little Saint Nick
4. At Christmas
5. Christmas
6. Rockin' Around The Christmas Tree
7. Christmas Time
8. Everybody Knows The Claus
9. Run Rudolph Run
10. Silent Night Medley
11. White Christmas
12. MMMBop (Live)
13. Madeline (Live)

Three Car Garage: The Independent Recordings . . . (Mercury)

1. Day Has Come
2. Two Tears

3. Thinking Of You—(Original Version)
4. River
5. Surely As The Sun
6. MMMBop—(Original Version)
7. Soldier
8. Stories
9. Pictures
10. Sometimes
11. With You In Your Dreams—(Original Version)

Live From Albertane (Mercury)

1. Gimme Some Lovin' / Shake A Tail Feather
2. Where's The Love
3. River
4 I Will Come To You
5. Ever Lonely
6. Speechless
7. With You In Your Dreams
8. A Minute Without You
9. Money (That's What I Want)
10. More Than Anything
11. MMMBop
12. Man From Milwaukee

This Time Around (Island)

1. You Never Know
2. If Only
3. This Time Around
4. Runaway Run
5. Save Me
6. Dying To Be Alive

7. Can't Stop
8. Wish That I Was There
9. Love Song
10. Sure About It
11. Hand In Hand
12. In The City
13. A Song To Sing

Singles

MMMBop

Where's The Love

I Will Come To You

Weird

Thinking Of You

This Time Around

Compilations

1998 Grammy Nominees (MCA)
MMMBop—Hanson

Now That's What I Call Music Vol. 1 (Virgin)
MMMBop—Hanson

Jack Frost (Soundtrack) (Mercury)
Good Lovin'—Hanson

Web Sites

**www.mercuryrecords.com/mercury/artists/hanson/
hanson_homepage.html**

www.hansonline.com

www.hanson.net

Fan Clubs

Hanson
c/o Island Records
825 Eighth Avenue
New York, New York 10019

Hanson
P.O. Box 703136
Tulsa, Oklahoma 74170

phone mail: (918) 446-3979

LFO

In a music scene dominated by boys, boys, boys, one group just can't stop singing about the girls, girls, girls that make their hearts beat fast especially when dressed in the requisite Abercrombie & Fitch. LFO is the hottest group out of the Trans-Continental Records camp, and perhaps that's because the guys that make up this trio just sizzle with sexiness and melt the hearts of adoring female fans.

Boston native Rich Cronin brings a fresh taste of hip-hop and rap to this boy band whose music clearly breaks the boundaries of traditional pop. Brad Fischetti's model looks push the band well into the pinup poster boy turf, but he's more than just another pretty face contributing amazing harmonies to the trio's repertoire. Devin Lima, with his out-of-control hair, injects his raw R&B vocals into the lead tracks of the group's melodic selections.

There's no dispute that LFO's sound stands out from

all the other bands—even their surrogate cousins at the Orlando hit factory where they were all hatched. Their music is a fresh harmonic combination of pop, rap, hip-hop, and R&B. "LFO is definitely different," says "Bow Legged" Lou George, the leader of R&B writing/producing team Full Force who has worked with the guys on several songs. "They're like a BBD, Bell-Biv-Devoe type thing because you got guys in there that are rapping and then you've got one lead singer, Devin. They're a different group than the Backstreet Boys."

"*Summer Girls* is just a totally different record than Backstreet Boys or 'N Sync," Rich agrees in an interview with *Billboard*. "It's really hip-hop with a Hootie & the Blowfish feel. We're just mixing hip-hop, rock, rap, and pop. Those other groups are going with a straight pop/R&B sound. It's not what we're about."

Clive Davis, president of Arista Records, told *Billboard*, "Backstreet Boys may be the target and the model, but what's very unique here is that Rich is writing these songs. These guys are raising the standard."

In fact, Rich wrote both of the group's first two hit singles, "Summer Girls" and "Girl on TV." "Girl on TV" was allegedly inspired by Jennifer Love Hewitt. The *Party of Five* star even appears in the song's video.

Rich has a habit of writing songs about pretty girls he knows. According to MTV News, "Summer Girls" was written as a tribute to the girlfriend he had when he was still in high school. "I haven't talked to her in a year or so," admits Rich. "I hope she does [hear it], though."

LFO's lyrics are quite unique in that they combine

phrases that don't go together simply for the sake of rhyme. In explaining "Summer Girls" lyrics to *Rolling Stone,* Rich said, "It's nonsense, but it's also about when you meet someone and get along real good, and it's a summertime thing, then they go home." It's a universal concept that young people growing up everywhere can certainly relate to.

What's particularly interesting about the lyrics are the two references to other classic boy bands. "New Kids On The Block had a bunch of hits . . ." pays tribute to fellow Bostonians Jordan and Jonathan Knight, Donnie Wahlberg, Danny Wood, and Joey McIntyre. And of course, "Love New Edition and the 'Candy Girl,' Remind me of you because you rock my world" pays tribute to the other Boston youth group of Michael Bivins, Bobby Brown, Ricky Bell, Ralph Tresvant, and Ronnie DeVoe.

In fact, indirectly, it was two former New Kids who gave LFO its name. The acronym stands for Lyte Funky Ones. According to *Rolling Stone,* Rich grew up with former New Kids Donnie Wahlberg and Danny Wood and they were all good friends. In fact, the members of NKOTB even helped him improve his songwriting skills. One day they christened him with the name Lyte Funky One. "It was a joke," Rich admits to the magazine. "Like Marky Mark and the Funky Bunch. But it goes somewhere and you're like, 'Wait a minute—I wish that wasn't what they called me.' "

Nonetheless, the name stuck. And so has the group. But the road to success wasn't without its dangerous curves and unforeseen potholes. Rich was visiting

Orlando when he first met Brad, an aspiring model/singer who hailed from New York. "I was always shy," Brad states on the group's official Web site. "I never danced at clubs, never did any talent shows. I just used to make up songs in the basement. Now I'm onstage in front of thousands of people. It's ridiculous! I love it!"

The two tall guys (they are both 6'3"), along with Brian "Brizz" Gillis started collaborating together and pumped out several dance tunes including "The Way You Like It" modeled after KC & the Sunshine Band's "That's the Way (I Like It)" and "Can't Have You" based on Yvonne Elliman's "If I Can't Have You."

The band was picked up by Trans-Continental and sent on tour with such acts as Backstreet Boys, 'N Sync, and LL Cool J. But early demands relating to dress code, personal issues, and the direction of the group left some doubts in their minds about whether they had made the right decision. What's more, their songs were performing way below their expectations.

"We felt unbelievable depression over the first two singles," Rich told *Billboard* of the lackluster response they received. "We were failing and incredibly unhappy, and we began to lose all our hope. We went through some trials and fights in the band." This led to the replacement of Brizz.

Soon after that, Brad and Rich met Devin, whose beautiful melodic vocals perfectly complimented LFO's edgier sound. At the time Devin was working as an employee of a department store. "When we got Devin, it added a sound that the group was missing," Rich continues. From there, LFO's music started to evolve from

dance to the hip-hop-based pop that has ultimately become their signature.

An early demo of "Summer Girls" was leaked to a radio station in Washington, D.C. The deejay liked what he heard so much that he played the unmastered demo live on the air. The song was so well received that a widespread buzz began to circulate. When the positive response reached its way back to the record company, they put LFO on the fast track to finish their album.

Days of disappointment appeared to be a thing of the past. Rich told *Teen People* that it was former New Kid Danny Wood's advice and encouragement that kept him going through the rough times. "The most profound thing Danny ever said to me in the beginning—and I should have listened to him—[was] make good music, love what you do, and everything will come."

As for Brizz, the former front man for LFO is now a solo artist reminiscent of Will Smith. He now goes by Mista Brizz and he too is signed with Trans-Continental Records, preparing for the release of his debut album.

Today the group's popularity is on the rise. They're touring the world with Britney Spears, and headlining their own show as well. Best of all, they're taking everything in stride and enjoying their success. Perhaps one day another band will pay homage to these guys by referencing LFO in a song. This gesture would not only bring the boys full circle, but it would also be the ultimate compliment.

Discography

Album

LFO (Arista)
1. Summer Girls
2. Girl On TV
3. Cross My Heart
4. Can't Have You
5. I Don't Wanna Kiss You Goodnight
6. West Side Story
7. Think About You
8. I Will Show You Mine
9. All I Need To Know
10. Baby Be Mine
11. Your Heart Is Safe With Me
12. My Block
13. Forever

Singles

Summer Girls

Girl On TV

Web Site

www.lytefunkieones.com

Fan Clubs

LFO Official Fan Club
P.O. Box 5127
Bellingham, Washington 98227

LFO
c/o Trans-Continental Entertainment
7380 Sand Lake Road, Suite 305
Orlando, Florida 32819

LFO
c/o Arista Records
Six West 57th Street
New York, New York 10019

feedback@lfo.com
brad@lfo.com
rich@lfo.com
devin@lfo.com

MDO

If you want to talk about being in the right place at the right time, look no further than South Beach in Miami, Florida, for MDO, the newest incarnation of legendary pop group Menudo. Capitalizing not only on the whole boy band phenomenon, but also on the surge of popular Latin crossover artists, MDO has all the odds in their favor with the release of their upcoming English album.

"English is a language that musically has no borders," notes Abel Talamantez, 22, a current member of MDO. "Latin people in the U.S. have always been in the music scene, and we have something different to offer. But it's like we're finally getting our chances. It's all a matter of our generation. We know English and Spanish because we've grown up in the United States. It was harder for my parents' generation to be in the music scene because they didn't know perfect English, and I think that shut doors for them."

Spanish-flavored Menudo was one of the original boy

bands. It was formed in 1977 by Edgardo Diaz who noticed a void in the music scene for this type of act. "All the music in our market was oriented for adults, and there was no music for teens or preteens," says the group's founder and manager, who created the all-male group after mild success with another Spanish teen band, La Pandilla. "That group was four boys and one girl. My experience was that the girl received letters saying that she was so lucky to be with the guys in the group. I realized that girls were more the potential market. That's why we came up with the idea of five boys in the band.

"At the beginning, a lot of people thought I was crazy," says Diaz, who got his start in the music business at age fourteen as a member of the traveling stage show *Up With People*. But after a successful twenty-year run, and tons of copycat acts, Diaz proved he wasn't crazy after all.

So far, there have been thirty-five members of Menudo/MDO. This is due in part to an unwritten rule that Edgardo Diaz created which mandated that once the boys reached a certain age (initially fifteen, later sixteen) they would be replaced. "The idea was to keep the group as teens," Diaz says. "After twenty years I decided that I wanted to change the concept and work in a different direction." This is why the guys currently in MDO are older, and have been with the group for a longer time.

The following list tracks the history of the group:

1. Nefty Sallaberry (1977–79) [original member, replaced by Rene Farrait]

2. Carlos Melendez (1977–80) [original member, replaced by Johnny Lozada]
3. Fernando Sallaberry (1977–80) [original member, replaced by Xavier Serbia]
4. Oscar Melendez (1977–81) [original member, replaced by Miguel Cancel]
5. Ricky Melendez (1977–84) [original member, replaced by Ricky Martin]

In 1987 Nefty, Carlos, Fernando, and Ricky regrouped to form the quartet Xchange.

6. Rene Farrait (1979–82) [replaced Nefty Sallaberry; replaced by Charlie Rivera]
7. Johnny Lozada (1980–84) [replaced Carlos Melendez; replaced by Robby Rosa]
8. Xavier Serbia (1980–83) [replaced Fernando Sallaberry; replaced by Ray Reyes]

In 1986 Rene, Johnny, and Xavier formed the trio Proyecto M, which recorded and toured through 1994.

9. Miguel Cancel (1981–83) [replaced Oscar Melendez, replaced by Roy Rossello]
10. Charlie Rivera (1982–87) [replaced Rene Farrait; replaced by Ralphy Rodriguez]
11. Ray Reyes (1983–85) [replaced Xavier Serbia; replaced by Raymond Acevedo]

In 1988 Ray replaced Xavier once again, this time as the new member of Proyecto M, alongside Rene and Johnny.

Ricky Melendez, Rene, Johnny, Miguel, Charlie and Ray are currently a part of the group, El Reencuentro.

12. Roy Rosello (1983–86) [replaced Miguel Cancel; replaced by Sergio Gonzalez]
13. Robby Rosa (1983–87) [replaced Johnny Lozada; replaced by Ruben Gomez]
14. Ricky Martin (1984–89) [replaced Ricky Melendez; replaced by Rawy Torres]

Robi Rosa (notice the new spelling of his name) and Ricky Martin have collaborated on Ricky's last three albums. Among the many songs Robi wrote and produced for Ricky are: "(Un, dos, tres) Maria," "La Copa de la Vida/The Cup of Life," and "Livin' la Vida Loca."

15. Raymond Acevedo (1985–88) [replaced Ray Reyes; replaced by Robert Avellanet]
16. Sergio Gonzalez (1986–90) [replaced Roy Rosello; replaced by Edward Aguilera]
17. Ralphy Rodriguez (1986–87) [replaced Charlie Rivera; replaced by Angelo Garcia]

Ralphy taped the pilot for *The New Mickey Mouse Club,* which spawned teen sensations Justin Timberlake, JC Chasez, Britney Spears, and Christina Aguilera. Unfortunately, Ralphy left after the pilot and was never a part of the show.

18. Ruben Gomez (1987–90) [replaced Robby Rosa; replaced by Jonathan Montenegro]

19. Angelo Garcia (1988–90) [replaced Ralphy Rodriguez; replaced by Cesar Abreu]
20. Robert Avellanet (1988–91) [replaced Raymond Acevedo; replaced by Ashley Ruiz]
21. Rawy Torres (1989–91) [replaced Ricky Martin; replaced by Andy Blazquez]

After the group broke up in '91, Robert, Rawy and three other guys created the group Euphoria.

22. Cesar Abreu (1990) [replaced Angelo Garcia; replaced by Adrian Olivares]
23. Adrian Olivares (1990–93) [replaced Cesar Abreu; replaced by Ricky Lopez]
24. Jonathan Montenegro (1990–91) [replaced Sergio Gonzalez; replaced by Alex Grullon]
25. Edward Aguilera (1990–91) [replaced Ruben Gomez; replaced by Abel Talamantez]
26. Ashley Ruiz (1991–95) [replaced Robert Avellanet; replaced by Didier Hernandez]
27. Andy Blazquez (1991–96) [replaced Rawy Torres; replaced by Danny Weider]
28. Alex Grullon (1991–present) [replaced Jonathan Montenegro]
29. Abel Talamantez (1991–present) [replaced Edward Aguilera]
30. Ricky Lopez (1993–95, 1998) [replaced Adrian Olivares; replaced by Anthony Galindo, MDO; 1998 replaced Danny Weider; replaced by Troy Tuminelli]

Ricky is the only ex-Menudo member to actually leave and return to the group.

31. Didier Hernandez (1995–present) [replaced Ashley Ruiz]
32. Anthony Galindo (1995–2000) [replaced Ricky Lopez; replaced by Poblo Portillo]

Alex, Abel, Ricky Lopez, Didier, and Anthony are the only ones to be part of both Menudo and MDO.

33. Danny Weider (1997–98) [replaced Andy Blazquez; replaced by Ricky Lopez]
34. Troy Tuminelli (2000–present) [replaced Ricky Lopez]
35. Pablo Portillo (2000–present) [replaced Anthony Galindo]

Danny, Troy and Pablo were never members of Menudo, only MDO.

The idea to change the name from Menudo to MDO originally came from the members of the group. "We wanted to change the name because we sort of felt for the English market, Menudo was something that had gone, like a brand name of clothes that had already gone out of style," says Abel. "We didn't want to do anything out of style, we wanted something different, so we invented it."

MDO's first self-titled album was actually going to be titled *Menudo*. "I think our manager and everybody

just knew it was time for change," says Abel. "We knew what we were doing music-wise and image-wise, but it wasn't really the essence of Menudo. We were already older and we sort of felt like Menudo was a little boys' group and we felt we had grown up."

"One of the motivations for us to change the name was because people sometimes just heard the name and thought that it was the sound and the songs from the 1980s," explains Diaz. "It was not. We were doing new stuff."

With a new name the group recorded two more Spanish albums. MDO's initial lineup included Abel, Alex Grullon, Didier Hernandez, Anthony Galindo, and Danny Weider. All the boys but Danny had previously been members of Menudo. When Danny left in 1998, he was replaced by another former member, Ricky Lopez. But Ricky's return to the group was short-lived and for a while, MDO performed as a quartet.

As any musical act knows, it's not always easy working as a group. "On a personal level, you have to respect each other. We respect each other a lot," says Abel. "We don't consider this just a business thing. We consider ourselves brothers. We listen to each other and we're there for each other as brothers and friends and when somebody has something to say, is going through problems, or wants to cry, we're there for him. We're family."

And because the group is so tight, it's awfully difficult when someone does decide to leave, like the latest exit, Anthony. Abel lets out a deep sigh when discussing the departure of his good friend. "It's very tough, 'cause

you have a friend and you establish an understanding and you share your dreams. I'm with those guys more than I'm with my blood brothers and sisters, and my parents. They become your family. It's like seeing a family member leave. It's not easy, but it's what I know. That's the business."

And Anthony truly is like family to Abel. If it wasn't for his fellow bandmate, Abel may not ever have met his wife, Natalie. "When he first joined the group, I started staying at his house just to get to know him," recalls Abel. "I started hanging out with him and meeting his friends from school. I was flipping through his yearbook and I saw this girl, a really pretty girl. I said 'Wow, this is it.' " Anthony made a phone call, and set up a date for his two friends. The rest is history.

"The one thing that never happened [in Menudo], happened to me . . . I got married by being in the group," explains Abel. "A lot of girls were kind of hurt, but I've always said everybody has the right to love and the right to make a family and be happy. I don't go around telling the fans you can't find love, you can't get married because you have to be faithful to the group. I think it would be a selfish point of view to take that attitude and prohibit someone from loving and feeling and being human."

Luckily, the fans understood and stood by Abel, writing many supportive letters when he tied the knot. Abel considers the birth of his daughter, Juliet, to be the highest high of his life. "As far as the group, I think just being here for what's coming up," he explains. "The highest high is yet to come, and it shall come. I defi-

nitely consider everything I've done up to now as very worthy, but I think it's for a purpose. It's like I've been in school, when you prepare yourself to be a doctor. I'm finally gonna go into the operating room and that's what's coming up for me."

After an international search, MDO has selected two new members to complete the group and bring them into the new millennium. The newest members to carry on the legacy are Troy Tuminelli and Pablo Portillo. Without a doubt, MDO will be around for another twenty years.

And don't discount the name Menudo quite yet, either. Several years ago Diaz sold the name to another company. Rumor has it that it was recently acquired by a new entity with plans to resurrect the group with all new kids. With the overall success of boy bands today, MDO and Menudo could very likely co-exist in the future.

Discography

Albums

MDO (Sony Discos)
1. No Puedo Olvidarme De Ti
2. Volveras A Mi
3. !Ay Amor!
4. !Ay Carino!
5. No Me Envenena Mas
6. A Bailar
7. Hablame De Amor

8. Subete A Mi Moto
9. Asi No Mas
10. Dame Una Caricia

Un Poco Mas (Sony Discos)
1. Dame Un Poco Mas
2. No Puedo Olvidar (Balada)
3. Baila La Rumba
4. Yo Solo Pienso En Ti
5. Diana
6. Tu Me Haces Sonar
7. Un Mundo Nuevo
8. Sera Por Eso
9. Toma Mis Manos
10. No Puedo Olvidar (Pop)
11. Groove With Me Tonight
12. Fantasy

Compilation

Music Of The Heart (Soundtrack) (Epic)
Groove With Me Tonight—MDO

Web Sites

www.mdo.org

members.aol.com/menudo77/frontpage.html

Fan Club

mdofan@mdo.org

Ricky Martin

The biggest success story ever to come out of Menudo is Ricky Martin. "I think that's one of the best things that has happened," concedes Menudo founder Edgardo Diaz. What's most impressive about this Latin legend is his pride in where he came from.

Backstage at the 1999 Billboard Music Awards, Ricky said, "I started a long time ago with a band." Of course, that band was Menudo. "I've surrounded myself with an amazing group of people—people I've been working with for fifteen years—people that know me well." People like collaborator and fellow ex-Menudo member Robi Rosa. "I want to do this for a long time, and the only way I can do this is by respecting myself and my beliefs and being faithful to them."

When Ricky was just starting out in Menudo, nobody had any idea he would become an international sensation. "Nobody knew, not even him," says Diaz, who described Ricky as a normal kid. "You always think you can be successful, but how big or how successful, you never know. He had been successful for a couple years, but at this level? Wow."

Current MDO member Abel Talamantez was lucky enough to hear Ricky's English album before anyone else. "He came over in his new Mercedes. He had just come from the studio and he wanted our opinion on a couple songs. I remember him having trouble putting on the CD because it was like a computer in there. He turned on every light in the car and pushed every button

before he could get that CD player working. He finally got it working and we heard it. It sounded great."

Abel and the rest of MDO aspire to follow in the footsteps of their famous predecessor. "Ricky is so focused, so determined to make it, and he's so talented," says Abel of his pal. "He's definitely made some right decisions in his life. He's very down to earth. He's never changed. He never will change. He's the same, no matter how much fame, no matter how much money. He definitely deserves what he's got."

But Abel reminds us that Ricky was not an overnight success. "He's been out there a while," Abel says. "I'm in those same shoes. I've been here waiting, my turn, for the longest time, so when I see somebody who's gone through that, you have to admire them for being so persistent and for going against the wave for so many years, and finally catching that big wave."

Knowing who you are and where you've come from has a big hand in long-term success. "Once you know your roots, you know who you are. Musically, [Menudo] is his roots. His roots are my roots. We come from the same school and he definitely learned that you stick to your roots because that's who you are. It's good to have history. We come from an organization that's been in the business for twenty years. I definitely know I wouldn't want to be anywhere else."

Web Site

www.rickymartin.com

Meaty Cheesy Boys

What started off as a single spot in a five-year-old ad campaign for burger chain Jack in the Box has suddenly taken on a life of its own. The Meaty Cheesy Boys were created as a tool for selling cheeseburgers, but their popularity has propelled them head on into the cutthroat world of boy bands. Complete with an official Web site, EJ, TK, JT, TJ, and the other EJ are taking a large bite out of the competition.

"We created the Meaty Cheesy Boys in response to the huge following of other boy bands and decided that if they could do it, we could too," explains Dick Sittig, who created the ad. "Actually, it wasn't that hard. There are a lot of teenage boys who are practicing this in the mirror at night, so it was pretty easy to find people." Through a casting call, five young men were chosen to fill the roles.

"Our main audience is young men, and we had a hunch that young men don't care for the boy bands, that

they might be a little jealous of their popularity with young girls," explains Sittig, who also wrote and directed the commercial. "We thought we could win over young men by making fun of these boy bands. What we didn't predict was that young girls would actually like the Meaty Cheesy Boys, not as a parody, but straight up."

This was not the first time Jack in the Box tried something like this. "We had done two spots for the Spicy Crispy Chicks two years ago which was a parody of the Spice Girls phenomenon," says Greg Joumas, Division Vice President of Marketing Communications for Jack in the Box. According to Sittig, however, that group has broken up forever. "Not unlike the Spice Girls, they've all gone their separate ways and pursued solo careers. Also, we don't make that sandwich anymore."

The Meaty Cheesy Boys took it up a notch when they surprised audiences by appearing on the 1999 Billboard Music Awards. "We kept it under wraps partially because we didn't want to have any of the boy bands that were being parodied to get all [annoyed] and flex their muscles before the show," explains Joumas. "But also because a lot of the humor was that it was a surprise. My God—these guys are really here."

Wade Robson portrays the other EJ when he's not working as Britney Spears's choreographer. "Britney was a little weird about it," the dancer reveals. "It was when she was doing the 'Crazy' video that I auditioned for the job. I mentioned it and it kind of went over her head. She didn't really know what the deal was. The

night of the Billboard Awards, I was in the trailer with her and we were talking about the performance that she was gonna do, and I told her I had to get dressed for the Meaty Cheesy Boys. She said, 'You're really doing that? Oh, that's mean.' "

But Wade, who is well connected in the teen music scene, never saw the act as mean-spirited. "The thing is, it kind of went past the parody thing. It kind of became its own thing," explains Wade. "I didn't really think it was so bad anymore. We weren't directly dogging on any particular group—just a parody on the whole idea of it."

Jack in the Box was extremely pleased with the show. "I think it went over really well, and I think their performance held up against the other acts," says Sittig. In fact, several artists referred to the Meaty Cheesy Boys throughout the remainder of the show, including the Dixie Chicks and Aerosmith. "Blink 182 and Jennifer Love Hewitt had their picture taken with them back stage," adds Joumas.

" 'N Sync loves it," reveals Wade, who has produced some music for the rival band. "They're messing with me constantly. Joey came up to me after the performance and said, 'It would have been great if you would have let us come up onstage and [mess you up] afterward.' "

Like many other popular teen icons, the Meaty Cheesy Boys have been linked to "scandal." Sources reveal that these flame-broiled burger babes might just be the Milli Vanilli of boy bands. "The people you see on TV are dancer/actors," reveals Joumas. "The singers are a completely different group."

Sittig is much more tight-lipped about the controversy. "Once you reach the top, I think everyone tries to take a shot at you and tear you down," he jokes. "I think that's an ugly rumor, probably put out by other boy bands. I think some boy bands are secretly envious and a little scared."

Wade sets the record straight. "We didn't sing at all—and that's the funny thing. We got record deal offers! Edmonds Entertainment—Baby Face—called us and offered us a production deal."

According to Sittig, there's been talk about TV and film deals as well. "We just had no idea that it would take off like this," he admits. "I hope there's more, but that remains in the hands of the boys and their agents."

Unfortunately, the Boys may be headed down the same path as their Spicy Crispy predecessors. "I don't think it's something that I'm gonna continue," reveals Wade. "It was fun for a moment, but I don't really want to be known as a Meaty Cheesy Boy."

Discography
Album
Meat, Cheese & Love
1. Meat, Cheese & Love
2. Ultimate Cheeseburger
3. No Burger, No Love
4. Your Love's Melting Me, Baby
5. With Or Without Buns
6. Cheeseless Nights
7. That's It

8. Drivin' Thru
9. The Love Song
10. It Just Isn't a Party Without Meat & Cheese
11. Ultimate Cheeseburger (Remix)

Web Site

www.meatycheesyboys.com

Fan Club

ej@meatycheesyboys.com
tk@meatycheesyboys.com
jt@meatycheesyboys.com
the.other.ej@meatycheesyboys.com
tj@meatycheesyboys.com

Wade Robson

Meaty Cheesy boy Wade Robson, better known as the other EJ, has a lot more on his mind than cheeseburgers. Consider this impressive list of accomplishments: He's a dancer, choreographer, music producer, director, rapper, and actor. Oh, and did I mention . . . he's only eighteen years old?!?

The Australian-born native started dancing at age two. At five he won a Michael Jackson look-alike contest and got a chance to meet his idol. This inspired him to get serious and join a dance company. Shortly there-

after, he moved to Los Angeles to pursue his craft. Wade contacted the king of pop, who took him under his wing, making the boy his protégé and casting him in such music videos as "Black or White" and "Heal the World."

At fourteen Wade became half of the rap duo Quo, who recorded an album for Sony. This allowed him the chance to choreograph the duo's videos, and similar opportunities followed, including Immature's "Stay the Night" video, Nickelodeon's tenth annual *Kids' Choice Awards*, and Walt Disney's *American Teacher Awards*. He's also done some work for artists Mandy Moore and Tyrese.

Wade has appeared in front of the camera as an actor in such films as *Kazam!* and *EdTV*, and on the television shows *Full House* and *Pacific Blue*. He's produced music for 'N Sync, Youngstown, and the title track for the movie *Mystery Men*.

His biggest break, however, was hooking up with pop sensation Britney Spears. He not only choreographs everything she does, but he's also directing her live tour and writing songs with the teen diva.

Wade initially met Britney through one of her dancers he had known. "He talked me up like crazy," explains Wade. "Nobody knew how old I was. She didn't know who I was at first. She just thought I was one of the dancers. We get to rehearsal, she realizes who I am, and takes the dancer in the corner and says, 'He's a baby, what are you doing?' But I showed her what we were doing and I proved myself. Right after I did that, she said, 'I want to sign you up for everything that I do.' "

For Wade the most exciting part is being able to put

everything together and then sit back and watch the final product. "I guess the most amazing thing was the first MTV Awards that we did in New York," recalls Wade. "I sat home and watched it on TV and realized what I just did in my living room has been broadcast to forty million people all over the world. To sit back and watch that is incredible."

While young Wade has accomplished more professionally than most do in a lifetime, this prodigy has only just begun. Ultimately, he'd like to direct films. "With the film thing, I can write and produce the music, I can do the score, I can write the film, I can direct the film, I can act in the film," says Wade. "Of course, not all at once. That would be too much to do."

The Moffatts

It may be a snow day, but school's still in session. High up in the mountains in beautiful Keystone, Colorado, snow glistens out the window of the Moffatts' vacation resort. While much of the week has been spent skiing, there is work to be done. Sure, writing new songs for their upcoming album is a definite priority, but first, the four brothers that make up this family band must finish their schoolwork. Home-schooled by their parents, the boys have just finished reading *Romeo & Juliet* by William Shakespeare. According to Dave, 16, one of the triplets, they actually read the play, and have not yet seen the Leonardo DiCaprio movie.

Learning at home and being on the road a lot may elicit sympathy from some adoring fans of this foursome that leads anything but a normal life. But please don't feel like they're missing out. "There are some things that we don't get to experience," admits Scott, 17, the oldest of the group. "But there are so many

experiences that we've already experienced that a lot of teenagers only dream of experiencing. We've been around the world three times now."

In addition to traditional subjects like math and English, the Moffatts also got a homemade lesson in music at a very early age. "Our family is a pretty musical family," explains Clint, not only a triplet, but also an identical twin. "Every day we'd wake up and have the music blaring to Bryan Adams, Led Zeppelin, or the Beach Boys."

"I learned to play by ear," explains Dave. "We all learned by ear. Our dad basically taught us three chords on every instrument, except on drums, of course. Other than that, we just picked it up and started playing."

And the boys sure can play. In fact, once they perfected their instruments, the guys decided to go out on tour and play the whole show themselves. "We let our backup band go and do their own thing," explains Clint. "We grabbed hold of all the instruments and played a two-hour show. We've been doing that for three years now."

Once the playing was perfected, songwriting became the next logical step. "We're all starting to get into the songwriting scene now," says Bob, the other identical twin. "Scott's been in there a long time because he sat down at a young age and was taught the basic songwriting techniques, so he's well educated on that stuff. Now all four of us are working with a lot of great songwriters, and they're teaching us a lot of great things so lyrically we all contribute a lot to the band."

"I don't think I've ever really written a song for which I've already had a planned-out idea," explains

Scott about his writing process. "I just pick up a guitar and start strumming a few chords. Then I start humming along and the lyrics come out. Hopefully I have a tape recorder there so I don't forget it."

Dave adds, "It's not hard to write songs, you just have to use your imagination."

When all the elements come together, audiences are treated to a great live show. "It's one of those things we really got into the business to do," says Clint. "You get to feel the audience, you get to hear the audience, you get to see the people that came out to watch you play, the people that buy tickets to hear you play your music. That's a really cool feeling that we love. You can do whatever you want. If you mess up, it doesn't matter because the crowd's not there to hear you mess up. They're there to have a fun time."

Seeing the boys perform live must bring an immense sense of pride to their parents, who play an active role in managing the family band. It wasn't too long ago that the family first moved into the basement of the boys' grandparents' home in Victoria, British Columbia. "They helped us out so much as far as getting us out there, letting us stay in their house, and letting us play music," says Bob. "They would just sit at the top of the stairs and listen to us play. They were very supportive of us getting to where we are right now."

Clint fondly remembers those early days. "We started up in Canada doing a lot of charity work. We'd go from senior home to senior home and just sing for people. That was really our goal—to make people happy with our music. It still is."

Some fans may not realize it, but the Moffatts started their musical career as a successful country act. When they were just little kids, they opened for fellow family band the Osmonds in Branson, Missouri. Dave remembers, "Wayne Osmond always said to pay your dues. Along the way people are gonna criticize you, and you just have to keep going. You think about it, and you think about what improvements you can make, but you don't take it right to the heart. People have their own opinions."

As the guys grew older, and their own listening tastes began to change, so did their desire to explore other musical styles as performers. "We decided, 'Why are we gonna play country music when we're listening to this other kind of music?' " explains Dave. "We just wanted to be happy with what we were playing. We knew that if we wanted to change, it would be all right with our fans. They gradually grew with it, too."

"Everyone can accept it because teenagers are always changing," says Scott. "We actually have a song on the album called 'Just Another Phase.' Every teenager goes through phases, goes through changes. For us, one of our major changes is music. Five years ago we were totally into Dwight Yoakam and Garth Brooks. Four years ago we were totally into Nirvana and Pearl Jam and Bush and Green Day. Now we're really influenced still by Nirvana, but also Radiohead and Blur and Robbie Williams, and stuff like that."

Scott considers himself an entertainer who loves to make music and wants to explore the outer boundaries of the medium. "You're gonna have something com-

pletely different all the time," he explains. "You're not gonna have a stereotype band. It's not gonna be the same thing over and over again."

One of the major things the Moffatts hope to accomplish is the ability to evolve with every album. "We want to reinvent ourselves as much as possible," explains Scott. "Elton John, the Beatles, all the great bands reinvented themselves after every album. After 'She Loves You' going to 'Sgt. Pepper's Lonely Hearts Club Band,' it wasn't really even the Beatles anymore. It was like a different band. That's something that we would always like to keep in mind."

While Scott does acknowledge that the Beatles may have lost some fans during that transition, he also notes that in the long run more people jumped on board because it was something different. "I think the Beatles were more accepted by the general public that way because they were real. They weren't a bunch of squeaky-clean school preppies. They were more like normal teenage guys making music, and that's what I think drew the audience into it."

One thing that transcends all musical phases is the status of teen idol. Girls just can't get enough of the four beautiful brothers. Of particular interest on fan sites across the Internet are the boys' funky hairstyles. "The different haircuts is just the way that we are," explains Clint, who sports a short cut with blond highlights in the front. "When we sang country music, we all had similar hairdos. We were going to the studio to record our country album called *The Moffatts,* and we went into the hair salon, looked at a book, and each guy

picked their own hairstyle. A few years later we said let's do something really weird to our hair, so this is how it ended up."

Scott, with his long blond hair, has always been a favorite among the female fans. He laughs off all the attention. "I think it was pretty cool for us to realize we made some sort of an impact on teenagers whether it be with music or hair."

The guys know that they're in a competitive business and image is extremely important. However, what's even more important to the guys is being real with their fans and themselves. "I think a lot of the boy groups out there are just making a false image of themselves because another band has made it with that type of image," says Bob. "For us it's all real. We go onstage with stuff that we've bought in the store that we've liked. If the fans like it, that's great, but the most important thing is that we like it."

Apparently the Moffatts do care what the fans think because they sometimes log onto the Internet to solicit their opinions. "We do a lot of chats with the fans because we want to know what their new things are and what they want to hear," says Clint.

Fans are very important to the boys. When a young girl with cancer told a newspaper that her one wish was to meet the Moffatts, the foursome flew to North Dakota to grant her wish. "We spent a day with her and we sang her a couple songs," says Bob. "That was kind of cool that one of her wishes was to meet the Moffatts. It makes me feel very special that we've impacted somebody's life. We know people need something in

their life to brighten up their days, so hopefully we've provided that for them."

Unfortunately, sometime the fans can get a bit too carried away. "We were in Spain," recalls Clint. "There was a lot of security on the main floor because there were three or four thousand people outside the hotel. We had the whole floor blocked off, and so we left our doors open. [We thought] 'There's enough security and nobody will ever get up here.' "

They won't make that mistake again. "I was getting my hair cut. We were basically just in our boxers—that was it," Clint continues. "All of a sudden this fan just walks into our room, breaks down, and starts crying. We said, 'Excuse me, you're gonna have to leave now. It's our personal time. We're in our hotel room, and this is not a good time.' She left and she started crying." It turned out she was the daughter of the hotel manager.

On top of everything else, the Moffatts share in the management responsibilities of their group. Bob handles publishing and record sales. Scott deals with songwriting and recording. Dave is in charge of endorsements and videos. Clint supervises marketing and merchandise. "When everything is brought to the table, we bring the whole family together and say, do we all agree upon this? Do we want to make any changes?" explains Clint. "That's pretty much how it works."

And it's worked very well up to now, and the band continues to flourish. In fact, the Moffatts hope to be around forever, constantly evolving, staying one step ahead of the game. "The Rolling Stones did it, so hopefully we'll be able to do it," notes Dave. "There was one

interview that we saw on the Rolling Stones, and [Mick Jagger] was asked if he was gonna play forever. He said, 'I'm definitely gonna play forever.' If you look at that now, you laugh because they're still playing forever, making albums." Perhaps, you'll read this again in twenty years and share a laugh with the Moffatts.

Discography

Albums

It's A Wonderful World
1. What A Wonderful World
2. Grandma
3. We're Off To The Rodeo
4. All I Have Is A Dream
5. Itty Bitty Smile
6. Bird Dog
7. I Think I'm Falling In Love
8. Dogs Is Dogs
9. Do Wah Diddy Diddy
10. That's All Right

A Moffatts' Christmas
1. Old Man Winter
2. The Brightest Star
3. Earl the Christmas Squirrel
4. The Greatest Gift
5. Santa's In My Neighborhood
6. How Would Jesus Feel
7. Oh What A Wonderful Day
8. Santa Knows

9. Christmas Eve
10. Santa Left A Hole In Daddy's Pocket

The Moffatts (Polydor Nashville)

1. I Think She Likes Me
2. This Boy
3. Guns Of Love
4. Mama Never Told Me 'Bout You
5. Just Thinkin' About You
6. When God Made You
7. Caterpillar Crawl
8. You Are What You Do
9. A Little Something
10. Don't Judge This Book

Chapter 1: A New Beginning (U.S.) (Capitol/EMI)

1. Until You Loved Me
2. Misery
3. Miss You Like Crazy
4. Written All Over My Heart
5. Girl Of My Dreams
6. Crazy
7. Say'n I Love You
8. Love
9. I'll Be There For You
10. Wild At Heart
11. Raining In My Mind
12. If Life Is So Short
13. Frustration
14. Over The Rainbow

Chapter 1: A New Beginning (Canadian/European)
(EMI)

1. Wild At Heart
2. Miss You Like Crazy
3. Say'n I Love You
4. Girl Of My Dreams
5. Crazy
6. Don't Walk Away
7. Now And Forever
8. Love
9. I'll Be There For You
10. Girl I'm Gonna Get You
11. We Are Young
12. If Life Is So Short
13. Jump

Upcoming Album Due Late Summer 2000

Singles

I'll Be There For You

Miss You Like Crazy

Crazy

If Life Is So Short

The Girl Of My Dreams

Until You Loved Me

Misery

Compilations

Teaching Mrs. Tingle (Soundtrack) (Capitol/EMI)
Misery—The Moffatts

Never Been Kissed (Soundtrack) (Capitol/EMI)
Until You Loved Me—The Moffatts

Web Sites

www.themoffatts.com

www.moffatthigh.com

Fan Clubs

The Moffatts Fan Club
P.O. Box 270337
Nashville, Tennessee 37227

Moffatts
c/o Capitol Records
1750 Vine Street
Los Angeles, California 90028-5274

98 Degrees

Las Vegas has always been considered an adult Mecca with its gambling casinos and burlesque stage shows. But as the home of the 1999 Billboard Music Awards, hardly a grown-up is in sight. Instead, throngs of kids fill the lobby of the MGM Grand Hotel, hoping to rendezvous with one of their favorite stars or recording artists. It's day for night inside the windowless hotel, but even if the fans staking out the lobby are aware that they've been waiting round the clock, they wouldn't trade their spot for a winning jackpot.

Early in the morning a blackjack dealer sees four young men running through the casino in their underwear. He has no idea who these guys are, so he asks one of the players at his table. "That's 98 Degrees," the player responds. "My daughter loves that group. She'll kill me if she knows she missed this spectacle."

Feeling as though he's had a personal brush with celebrity, the dealer proudly tells all who sit at his table

throughout the remainder of the day of that morning's exploits. A buzz reverberates throughout the casino, many girls nearly fainting when they learn they missed the chance to see Nick Lachey, Drew Lachey, Justin Jeffre, and Jeff Timmons running around in nothing but their boxer shorts. Word leaks to the Vegas strip, and by noon that same day, three times as many camera-toting fans inhabit the lobby.

Los Angeles radio personality JoJo Wright of KIIS-FM explains it best. "What do [the fans] want? They want backstage. That's crème de la crème." For his nightly broadcast Wright has created an in-studio audience where he crams lucky fans into the studio whenever he has a guest artist stop by. "It's better than a backstage party. These guys shake their hands, maybe take a picture, a little chat here and there depending on how much time we're not on the radio. People in general really seem excited to be a part of this whole thing."

The night that 98 Degrees visited Wright's show was really crazy. "We brought the 98 Degrees guys in underneath the building," he recalls. "Security at the building hated me at that point. There were listeners all over the place, surrounding the building. They rush around to try and find the place [the guys are] coming in through. Finally they show up. The place goes nuts. We brought them upstairs. We have the listeners that won the tickets sitting in one room. I bring the group in. They all go insane."

The building was set up so there were live radio speakers on the ground so the fans outside could hear what was going on. They broadcast from a conference

room with large glass windows so those that didn't win seats in-studio could still see the guys. "We all had headphones on, and we could hear the crowd over the live mike from downstairs," explains Wright. "I said, 'Hey, you guys, what's going on?' And I heard this yell in my headphones [roar of crowd]. I introduced Nick, and Nick walked over and hopped in the window, and we heard the crowd go nuts downstairs. They're looking up seeing us as clear as day in the window. All I can see down is flashes. It was really awesome. I hope it came across on the radio half as much as it did in person."

And how do the guys react to this kind of attention? "I think a lot of them are really flattered by it," admits Wright. "A lot of times when they come in, they're really tired. They get run ragged and pulled in a lot of directions. But usually when they see the reactions of the people, they get pumped up."

Wright advises fans to just be respectful of the artists. "If they get an autograph, great. If you ask them for their ninth autograph for your cousin in Alabama, it can get a little tiring. They seem to like meeting good people who appreciate their work. I wouldn't suggest jumping on them and pulling a piece of their hair out to show your cousin that you've got a piece of Nick's hair. He may not appreciate that as much."

The respect works both ways. "Being respectful of other people . . . will get you farther than singing your face off," Drew told *Teen People*.

Nick told fans in an online chat on react.com, "You have to make certain adjustments, your personal life isn't quite as personal anymore, and you have to be pre-

pared for that. [But] we're always excited to meet our fans and it's all very flattering."

"We find it hard to believe that anyone would like us," Justin told *Teen People*. "We look at ourselves as the same old goofballs that we were when we started."

"I'm the same person I was before, and I don't want to be treated any differently," adds Jeff.

It's hard to imagine bad boy Nick, cool cat Justin, pinup hunk Jeff, and baby-faced Drew as normal everyday guys; but they truly were just regular folk. Jeff, Nick, and Justin were classmates at the Cincinnati School for Creative and Performing Arts. After finishing school, Jeff moved to Los Angeles to pursue his musical interests. He decided to form a band and called upon his fellow alums, Justin and Nick. Nick's younger brother Drew left a job as a medical technician in Brooklyn to complete the group. 98 Degrees was born.

The guys' big break came when they crashed backstage at a Boyz II Men concert. They sang a cappella to the group's manager. Once he heard their amazing vocal abilities, and complex blend of tantalizing harmonies, he signed them to Motown Records on the spot. This was a huge deal for the group to be signed onto an R&B—not pop—label.

Now that they've made the big time, there's no looking back. "Probably the biggest drawback of this career [is] being away from our friends and family," Jeff told react.com. "But the perks are awesome, getting to go all around the world and meeting cool people."

Because they are four gorgeous guys who can sing, 98 Degrees has been given the obvious label by the

media. "We don't really consider ourselves a boy band because we're too old for that," Jeff insisted to react.com.

Justin tries to nail down how they are different from the other guy groups: "I think it's definitely the music. We have a very mature sound, very harmony based. We do a lot of writing and producing ourselves. And we're very hands on with our music whereas some of the other groups are more into dancing and stuff. And that's cool. We're just different. I think once people come to a 98 Degrees concert, and listen to our albums, they can really see the difference."

"98 Degrees is a little more polished and a little less likely to do 'Larger Than Life,' and more likely to do 'Back To Your Heart,' " notes Gary Baker, who has written several songs for the guys, including "If Every Day Could Be Christmas" for their holiday album. "When I see 98 Degrees live, I'm blown away by them."

It's very much a consensus within the music industry that the most important element to any musical act is the song. Groups are defined by the songs they perform.

Country singer/songwriter Keith Stegall wrote the song "I Do (Cherish You)," which 98 Degrees made into a hit. But the song was not initially intended for the pop market! "[Co-writer] Dan Hill and I had taken a little vacation down to Nassau to do some writing," Stegall explains. "I got up one morning and came up with the title and then started playing around with the melody and had a chorus worked out and part of the verse."

Stegall was so excited by his progress on the tune

that he called Hill into the room to help him come up with some lyrics. "He's such an unbelievable lyricist," says Stegall. "He [loves] words and the use of words, like I do music and composing. So I was able to give him what I had and he of course bought into it and got inspired and took a rough tape copy of the framework of what I had put together and said 'Let me go work on this for a while.' "

Hill disappeared into his room for about two hours. When he returned, he had finished a rough sketch of the remainder of the song that the guys honed until "I Do" was completed. "We wrote about four songs together on that trip, and it was the last song that we wrote before we came back," Stegall remembers. "I'm always surprised by that. You can plan, but it's always the stuff that falls out at the last moment that seems to work."

Ironically, Stegall's inspiration to pen the tune was sparked by a really nasty divorce. "I had met someone who kind of restored my faith in relationships," explains Stegall. "That had a lot of impact on me. I remember sitting down that morning to write, and I thought, you know, I just want to write a song that's positive and about how a relationship, when it's good and you're in love with somebody, where all those emotions come from. In the back of my mind I thought, this has got to be ultra simple, too. I've always found for me, the most simple, direct things are the things that always seem to work because they're the things that people can immediately grasp and relate to."

The completed song was initially recorded by country artist Mark Wills. Bruce Carbone, at Universal

Records, was in Nashville looking for songs, and he'd been through a lot of different writers in town. "A lot of times it's always the same thing," says Stegall. "It's pop music—you're not gonna find what you want in Nashville, but he was persistent because he felt that it was a songwriter's town and he might find something. So when he was in my office, I of course played him the Mark record and he goes, 'That's perfect! That's what I'm looking for for 98 Degrees.' So I pulled the demo out that Dan and I had made, and that's what he took back to New York with him."

Stegall already knew of 98 Degrees because of "Invisible Man," their hit single on the first album, but they were still basically a baby act. "I was aware of what they had done and that they were into their second album and that this would hopefully be the album that broke them through," recalls Stegall.

When Stegall heard 98 Degrees' cover of the song, it was magic. "The only other time I had that kind of feeling about something I had written was when I first heard 'We're in this Love Together' when Al Jarreau had done it and I knew immediately, 'They've hooked it. This is gonna be a big record.' I've had records before where I just didn't feel that the artist pulled the song off, but then I've had situations like this with 98 Degrees where the singers, the artists brought something to it that took it to another level, that made the lyrics even more believable than it would have been. That's always a thrill to me. The biggest kick in the world out of everything I've done is to be driving down the road and hear something that I thought up

that's been put to music that's beaming out across the world."

98 Degrees truly has a gift for making beautiful music. They consider themselves blessed. "You just have to put everything into proper perspective, and look at what we're doing as a gift and an opportunity that most people don't have," Jeff said in an online chat. "And to keep in mind that whoever gave us this opportunity can quickly take it away if it gets to our head."

Thankfully the guys are well grounded, and they count on each other to remain firmly planted. "It can be very stressful, but we try to be there for each other," Jeff tells *Teen People*. "We give each other a hard time to make each other laugh."

"I think the experiences we've gone through as a group, both bad and good, have strengthened our friendships," Nick told react.com. "So success is something we've all enjoyed together and has been strengthening."

Nick and Drew have been singing together longer than any of the others. That's because these brothers grew up singing. "[Drew] and I have a good relationship, and we're more like best friends than brothers," Nick said in an online chat. "And the other guys are more like brothers than best friends, so it's all mixed up!"

A lot of media focus lately has been on Nick's blossoming relationship with fellow singer Jessica Simpson. It began when they toured together last year and performed a duet onstage called "Where You Are." The

song is featured on the soundtrack of the film *Here on Earth* starring Chris Klein.

"The duet was a lot of fun," says Nick. "It's a lot of fun working with her. She's a great, great singer and a real pleasure." But don't worry about this handsome hunk going solo any time soon. "Solo work? Nah, I'm just concentrating on 98 Degrees. We're just having such a good time doing what we do as a group that I can't really say that there's anything in the works for that."

For now, Nick and the guys just continue to do what they do best, not letting anything get in their way or distract them from their common goal. He offers the following advice to young fans, "Follow your dream in life whatever it may be. Have faith and work toward your goals and believe it can happen to you."

Backstage at the Billboard Awards, 98 Degrees marches down the red carpet to thunderous applause and screams by adoring fans who've moved from their precious spot in the lobby to the cold concrete just behind the theater. It's time to confront the boys about the now infamous underwear incident.

"Well, since we didn't get in till about noon," says Drew, "we probably weren't walking around in our underwear this morning."

Another rumor squashed.

The show opens with a parody of Blink 182's "What's My Age Again?" with the band running naked through the casinos in Vegas à la their famous flesh-exhibiting video. The culprits are finally nailed.

Discography

Albums

98 Degrees (Motown)

1. Intro
2. Come And Get It
3. Invisible Man
4. Was It Something I Didn't Say
5. Take My Breath Away
6. Hand In Hand (Duet w/ LaShandra Reese)
7. Intermood
8. Dreaming
9. Heaven's Missing An Angel
10. I Wasn't Over You
11. Completely
12. Don't Stop The Love
13. I Wanna Love You

98 Degrees & Rising (Motown)

1. Intro
2. Heat It Up
3. If She Only Knew
4. I Do (Cherish You)
5. Fly With Me
6. Still
7. Because Of You
8. Give It Up (Interlude)
9. Do You Wanna Dance
10. True To Your Heart
11. To Me You're Everything
12. The Hardest Thing
13. She's Out Of My Life

This Christmas (Universal)
1. If Every Day Could Be Christmas
2. God Rest Ye Merry Gentlemen
3. The Christmas Song (Chestnuts Roasting On An Open Fire)
4. I'll Be Home For Christmas
5. Oh Holy Night
6. This Gift
7. Little Drummer Boy
8. Christmas Wish
9. Silent Night
10. Ave Maria
11. This Gift (Pop Version)

Singles

Invisible Man

Because Of You

The Hardest Thing

I Do (Cherish You)—Radio Only Release

This Gift—Radio Only Release

Compilation

Notting Hill (Soundtrack) (Island)
I Do (Cherish You)—98 Degrees

Web Site

www.98degrees.com/index.html

Fan Clubs

Worldwide 98 Degrees Fan Club
P.O. Box 31379
Cincinnati, Ohio 45231

98 Degrees
c/o Universal Records Inc.
1325 Avenue of the Americas
New York, New York 10019

No Authority

Inside an abandoned building, at a top-secret Hollywood location, four guys clown around posing for a series of publicity stills. While most of their friends are stuck at school listening to teachers drone on about math and English and stuff like that, this tight group is hard at work modeling for the cover of their upcoming album. Algebraic equations and iambic pentameter are not of concern to these photogenic fellas. Instead, they debate much more pressing issues like which CD they should listen to: Beastie Boys or Fiona Apple.

Meet No Authority: Eric Stretch, a tall, lanky sweetheart whose dark hair and pale skin make his eyes shine like stardust; Ricky G, a self-proclaimed perfectionist who is a bundle of energy and a consummate professional all wrapped up into one smooth package; Danny Zavatsky, the surfer/skater dude your mom always warned you about—but somehow his shy smile melts away any parent's fears and captures every girl's heart;

and Tommy McCarthy, a tough-looking smart guy with bad-boy tattoos, piercing blue eyes, and a voice that makes you want to fall in love.

But don't let their looks fool you. The patient photographer soon discovers how the group earned their name. Ricky, who came up with the moniker, explains, "No Authority means that the authority is you. It's not the person next to you. It's not your neighbor. It's not your best friend. We do things the way we want to do them."

Because Ricky is loudest, Fiona soon fills the room. But after a few minutes, Danny and Tommy beg their publicist to change the CD. Eric remains neutral throughout, as his musical tastes are the most eclectic of the band. After a few tracks of Beastie Boys, the guys compromise on something everyone will appreciate: Limp Bizkit. And with the sounds of Fred Durst blaring through the speakers, the boys start dancing and moshing, singing along and having a great time. As if on cue, the photographer starts snapping away.

Watching the guys jump around and bang into one another is a far stretch from the neatly polished, carefully choreographed stage shows they perform live on tour. The soundtrack of alternative rock is quite jarring if one is expecting the infectious melodies, smooth harmonies, hard-driving beats, and heartfelt ballads of the group's own first two albums. However, what isn't disguised is an incredible energy and love of performance that transcends everything else.

For Danny, the youngest member of the band, performing in front of a live audience is what he loves

most. "That's our main place to shine. When we're onstage we just tear it up and give it our all. It's insane to see all the girls out there actually screaming over you. It's nothing you've ever felt before."

Hearing his name screamed by thousands of adoring fans is exactly the kind of rush that pumps up this teen heartthrob. "Whatever I can do to get a genuine rush," Danny explains. "Surfing big waves gets the biggest rush. Snowboarding down big hills and hitting big jumps, skateboarding behind cars, anything that keeps my adrenaline going just to get me excited."

Sometimes this thrill-seeker gets himself into embarrassing situations. "We had to streak across the field during halftime while the girls were playing soccer," recalls Danny about a club initiation in high school. "We had to take off our underwear . . . and run [naked] across the field. We had to climb the fence, jump over, and hop in our buddy's car. He took off, but we [ultimately] got in trouble."

Keeping their clothes on seems to be a recurring problem for this group of sexy young hunks. As a child, Eric played soccer on a traveling team. After winning a tournament that they were expecting to lose, he threw a pool party to celebrate the team's victory. "There were a lot of people there and we were having diving contests," Eric remembers. He screamed for everyone to watch him do a flip off of the diving board. "Right when I said that, everyone's head turned, and my friend behind me pantsed me and I wasn't wearing any underwear." He quickly jumped in the pool and swam underwater to hide his embarrassment.

Ricky is not immune to these disconcerting moments of nakedness, either. He recalls, "I was taking a shower after a show, and they grabbed my stuff and put it on the tour bus so I had nothing [to wear]." Ever the accomplished prankster, Ricky decided to get back at his bandmates. He put on a bright orange pair of Reebok shoes that had been used in the act, wrapped a small towel around his waist, and marched outside.

"He walked out of the arena with just a towel on and then he took it off," recounts a shocked Eric.

"All the girls were outside and they were screaming," adds a confident Ricky. "The guys were so embarrassed. I just loved it."

But the band is so much more than just a group of pinup-poster pretty boys. "Ricky has such a passion for music," says Eric of his friend. In fact, music is the one hobby that this diverse group actually has in common.

Ricky and Tommy have begun writing songs together. One of these songs, "Thinkin'," made it onto the band's second CD. They're already collaborating on new tunes for the future. For their third installment all the guys plan to ramp up their musical involvement. "All of us are going to be playing instruments on the next album," reveals Tommy, who played drums at his church for five years. "Ricky's going to be playing guitar. Eric on keyboard. Danny is going to learn bass."

Not bad for a group of struggling child actors who began singing together just for fun. At a party a manager overheard the friends casually singing "Happy Birthday" and signed them on the spot. "I didn't know what I was getting myself into," claims Eric. "It was

always just something that was so fun to me. I never understood the pressures of 'I have to get a record deal or otherwise we're not going to make it.' "

But they did make it. Their manager brought them to the attention of superstar Michael Jackson. This legendary man in the mirror just couldn't stop till he got enough of this bad boy band. And the rest, of course, is history.

"I was just going with the flow," says Eric. When he learned that the king of pop was going to sign No Authority to his personal record label, Eric's first thought was "Oh my God, I'm gonna be famous. This is way too much for me."

The group initially consisted of Eric, Ricky, Danny, and fellow child actor Josh Keaton. Tommy joined the band later when Josh left to pursue other interests. At the time, Tommy, the band's only non-Southern California native, was working behind the scenes at the recording studio where No Authority laid down their tracks. He would see them around and he always thought they were pretty cool, but he never imagined in his wildest fantasies that one day he would be part of the group.

"I was just planning on being a producer or writer and putting together groups," says Tommy, who hails from South Carolina. "When they asked me to join them, I was like, why not? I've done the business side for a little while. Now I want to try and hop over and do the performing thing because being onstage is really what I love."

It wasn't easy at first. The fans missed Josh and gave Tommy a lukewarm reception. "The fans just didn't

understand that it wasn't like he was being replaced. Josh decided to leave," explains Tommy. "I would go on the Internet all the time and try to defend myself: 'I'm not trying to take his place, I'm just doing my thing.' "

Once the fans recognized Tommy's amazing talents, they quickly softened. As everyone now knows, Tommy is a perfect fit and an integral part of No Authority. "You can ask the guys, we are a much tighter group now and we're all really happy," says Tommy. "It's more like a family—we're brothers."

Like all brothers, the boys have disagreements from time to time. "Being that I'm a Pisces, I like to look at both sides of every issue," says Tommy, the band's oldest member. "In the group I do the same thing. I'm always the moderator. I would know what kind of argument somebody would have for something and I'd be prepared to respond to anything that they would throw at me." These skills may be why Tommy has always dreamed of going to Harvard to study law.

One thing they don't have to fight over are the ladies, as all of the guys have different tastes in women. Ricky, who likes his sweetie to call him "love muffin," looks for poise in his mate. "Not overly confident, but just confident and sweet. She has to shower me with attention because I always need to have reassurance that she likes me." He enjoys going online and checking out fan pages because there are great pictures of him and the fans together that he's never seen. "It's a good way to meet all your fans intimately."

The guys agree they would each date a fan—if she were the right one. "I would love to go out with a fan,"

reveals Eric. "There's definitely got to be a physical attraction. But for me to want to pursue more, it's all about the attitude. She's got to be friendly, outgoing, and funny. If there's a fan that I connect with and bond with, that would be great."

Tommy advises, "Approach me as a person, not as a fan. I understand the fact that a lot of people wouldn't know who we were if it wasn't for what we do. But it's a job. We just have more exposure than most other jobs. If it's the right person and they aren't all caught up with what we do, if they just talk about everyday things with us, and if we can get along with them on a personal level, then there's really no problem. I think we all agree if the right person came along, then yes, we would date a fan."

Danny warns fans that might be interested in dating him not to come up to him and start squealing. "It's kind of hard to talk to somebody when they're screaming the whole time. I don't like when girls feel like that. I just want girls to be comfortable around me. What if I worked at [the grocery store] or something like that— you wouldn't do that. Just because I'm a singer, I'm still a normal person. Just act like yourself and don't hold me in any higher stance than you would anyone else. I'm just a normal kid trying to have fun."

And like other normal kids, fame does not make Danny immune from the realities of life. When his parents split up a few years ago, he had a hard time at first. "Don't blame it on yourself," advises Danny from his own experiences. "That's what I did. My mom had to come out to L.A. every day while I auditioned for stuff,

and I always thought that it was my fault they split up because I was always taking up their time so they could never be together."

He soon learned that this wasn't the case at all. "Just stay strong, and it will work out," he advises. What helped Danny get through this rough patch in his personal history were the guys in the band because they were always there for him. "Me and the guys are like best friends."

The photo session is almost over. The photographer asks the guys to come up with a funny pose. Without hesitation, they drop their pants and smile for the camera. These guys just can't ever seem to keep their clothes on. But there is no embarrassment. There is no shame. They do what they do because they make the rules. No one else will ever tell these boys what they can and cannot do because there simply is No Authority.

Discography

Albums
Keep On (MJJ)
1. Don't Stop
2. Up And Down
3. Girlfriend
4. Why
5. She Drives Me Crazy
6. Please Don't Break My Heart
7. Keep On
8. One More Time
9. If You Want Me

10. Never Let You Go
11. I Like It

No Authority (MJJ)
1. Here I Am
2. I'm Telling You This
3. What I Wanna Do
4. Beautiful Girl
5. Can I Get Your Number
6. Don't Get Better
7. Don't Go
8. Never Had A Lover
9. Make You Dance
10. Thinkin'
11. I Can't Go On

Singles

What I Wanna Do

One More Time

Compilation

Trippin' (MJJ)
Girlfriend—No Authority

Web Site

www.noauthority.com

Fan Clubs

No Authority Fan Club
P.O. Box 1668
Hollywood, California 90078

No Authority
c/o Smash Music
6464 Sunset Boulevard
Hollywood, California 90028

Josh Keaton

Leaving No Authority was one of the hardest decisions Josh Keaton has ever made. The University of Southern California (USC) sophomore left the group for a few different reasons. "I wanted to be able to finish college. I also wanted to continue acting," explains Josh. "Everybody always has their vision of where everything should be going, and there were some creative differences between the management and myself. But I left the group on good terms with the guys."

Despite their busy schedules, Josh tries to stay in touch with his former bandmates. In fact, the day after this interview, Josh had plans to hang out with Danny. "Danny actually knew for a while that I wanted to leave," says Josh, who first notified management that he would officially no longer be part of the group. "When I did that

there wasn't anything scheduled for at least two months. Then I called Danny that same day and I said, 'I officially did it, I officially quit.' He had to stop for a second. He just couldn't believe that I did it. With Eric and Ricky, I said, 'This is what I need to do and I wish you guys the best of luck with the second album. I still want to hear how everything sounds. I still want to support you.'

"There were rumors going around that I let the guys down," says Josh. "That hurts because I did my best not to do anything to let them down. I waited to leave until I knew that we weren't going to be promoting the *Keep On* album anymore, because there's always an interim when you stop promoting one album before you even start recording the new album. I gave them enough time so that they could find another member."

Josh knew adding a new member once he left was inevitable. "I knew that was gonna happen. It's got to happen. Once I left, I knew there was gonna be a replacement. In a way, I think [Tommy] had to go through a lot in the beginning, because he had to prove himself to all the people who said, 'You're just trying to replace Josh.' I can't even imagine what that must be like. But he did it, and that deserves respect."

In the meantime, Josh is trying to earn his own respect as a solo artist. After leaving the group, Josh signed with mega-manager Johnny Wright, who helped him secure a record deal for his self-titled debut album. "You have to be a lot more self-motivated because everything relies on you," says Josh about working solo. "It's not like there's three other guys who are also the subject of everybody's attention. When you're a solo act,

everybody's gonna be looking at you. Even the days at the studio are much longer and much harder because you're doing everything yourself."

Working alone has also freed up valuable time for Josh to finish his studies and pursue his acting career. "Music and acting should be able to work in conjunction with each other because one thing can only complement the other. Look at Ricky Martin [*General Hospital*]." With Josh's ambition and determination, it won't be long before he too is livin' la vida loca and playing to sold-out audiences around the globe.

'N Sync

Any fan of 'N Sync can easily recount the story of how these five young talents first got together . . . Chris Kirkpatrick wanted to form a vocal group. He and Joey Fatone were working together at Universal Studios theme park in Orlando, Florida. Through a mutual friend, Chris met Justin Timberlake, a former star of the *Mickey Mouse Club*. Justin's friend and co-star on the show was JC Chasez. The boys hit it off and started singing as a quartet, but something was missing from the mix. Justin's vocal coach recommended Lance Bass, who, ironically, had a beautiful deep bass voice that rounded out the group's sound. Soon thereafter, the quintet was noticed by Trans-Continental Records, the same hit factory that launched the Backstreet Boys. Suddenly things started happening for the group at warp speed.

"When we put our group together—and we were together for about six months before we met Johnny

[Wright]—I didn't even know who the Backstreet Boys were," Justin told *Teen People*. Wright, of course, is the group's manager who previously handled Backstreet Boys and initially started out in the business as a tour manager for the New Kids on the Block.

Before things heated up, the guys would take advantage of any opportunity they could grab, just to perform and perfect their craft. "We'd perform for whoever would listen," Justin told *Entertainment Weekly*. "We'd be in the middle of a restaurant saying, 'Can we sing for you?' "

Their hard work and dedication has definitely paid off. Their self-titled debut album has already gone platinum more than ten times! "I look at 'N Sync and think those [guys] have got the world [in their hands]," observes former New Kid Joey McIntyre. "They're blessed with a friendship that seems like they're in it together, they're having fun, they've got a lot of energy, they seem to know what it's all about. And plus, they're very talented."

Director Lionel C. Martin agrees. "These guys are real talented and have a certain amount of charisma about them." Martin has directed videos for many of the teen pop groups. In fact, he's worked with 'N Sync repeatedly, helming such videos as "God Must Have Spent A Little More Time On You" and "You're Drivin' Me Crazy."

KIIS-FM radio personality JoJo Wright attended the 2000 American Music Awards and witnessed the band's brilliant show firsthand. "I was really impressed by their performance. They were sharp, very in sync," laughs the deejay. "They really knocked them dead—no question

about it. Things like that keep a group going. They put a lot of work into it."

A few days later Wright had a chance to speak to Lance about their nationally televised performance. "Lance said Tommy Lee came up to them backstage and said, 'Dude, you guys were awesome.' And that's two different worlds talking right there." Tommy Lee, Mr. Bad Boy of Motley Crue, complimenting all-American, sweet-as-apple-pie Lance Bass. "That's just not expected."

The thing that keeps the guys on track the most is the love and support of their fans. "[The fans] appreciate what you do because you love to do it," Justin told the *London Free Press*. "And that makes them love it."

The guys have a lot of faith in their fans and they're willing to do whatever they can to show their thanks. "We're very trusting," Chris told *Entertainment Weekly*. "If you give us the shirt off your back, we're gonna give you the shirts off our backs—plus our pants."

Some fans take those sentiments a bit too literally. "We have fans who know my underwear size," Justin told *Entertainment Weekly*. "People come up with signs that say 'JC, Drop Your Pants'—That's funny to us."

Because the guys have been performing since they were little kids, they try to encourage other young people to get in touch with their creative side. "I know from my own experiences that music gives kids a way to channel their energy and emotions into something positive," Justin said at a Washington, D.C., elementary school, according to *US Newswire*. "It's so important for kids to have the chance to find what they're good at

in school, and feel like they're a part of the system, and music is something that can make that happen in a creative and exciting way."

Perhaps this is one of the reasons the band was drawn to the movie *Music of The Heart* and agreed to record the film's theme song as a duet with Gloria Estefan. Nigel Dick directed the video for the movie's title track. "They've made a record with Gloria Estefan. They've never met Gloria. Gloria's never met them. But they're both on the record together. They've both recorded their tracks in different parts of the country."

Of course, when the guys from 'N Sync finally met the Latin diva on the set of the video, they hit it off immediately. Because the schedule on a video shoot is so tight, and there's a lot of work to be done, there's often not much time to socialize. "With a lot of bands like an 'N Sync, you never really get a chance to find out what they're like," says Dick, who has directed videos for all the top teen acts.

Sometimes a group will work repeatedly with the same director. Such is the case with Lionel C. Martin. "I think the key to my success is being able to incorporate the ideas of the groups in making the video. When you do that, they come back to you because they feel that this guy really represented our idea. It's a collaborative thing. You have to listen to the artist and make them feel that I'm doing to the best of my ability with whatever budget to make something that they feel good about."

One of Martin's most memorable experiences was directing the video for "God Must Have Spent a Little

More Time on You." "They sat down in a room with me and they had ideas," recalls Martin. "They said, 'We want something we can show our mom. We want to show the relationship between mom and child, that's kind of important.' It was their idea of going oldies. I thought that was refreshing and kind of nice."

Martin listened to their thoughts and came up with the concept of using a movie projector. "I said, let's have this projector that's rolling and the mom is sitting down, she's older now and she's watching the scenes of her growing up with her kid, almost like a family movie kind of thing. That to me is giving it a little bit of an edge and the projector is always cool because I'm a visual person and I'm always thinking about MTV and doing a video that's really a hot-looking clip.

"If you just take exactly what the artist says, which is what some directors do, then you can hurt yourself too, so you have to bring it to another level," continues Martin. "I think if I listened to them all the way, they would not have been in the video! I thought about this idea of them being dressed in white, almost like angels, coming in and out of the video. Basically, that collaboration—telling them my ideas and basically enhancing a vision that they already had, it just turned out to be a very hot-looking clip. They were very pleased and very happy and that's a good example of how a collaboration works."

The music video is an integral selling tool in today's music industry. This is one of the reasons image has become so important, especially for boy bands like 'N Sync. Music industry insiders consider Chris

Kirkpatrick to be one of the brightest guys in the business when it comes to image.

"Chris is a pretty smart guy," says Wright, also known as JoJo on the Radio. "When 'N Sync first started, they were just five young guys—nobody knew who they were. For some reason, I don't know if by accident, or his own little plan, but Chris put the little braids in his hair. He wasn't the stud boy of the group— that was clearly going to be Justin and JC. But the braids made Chris stand out.

"For people who didn't know the group inside and out, that's the first one they'd recognize," Wright continues. "You walk through the mall, five guys, that's the one you pick out. I think he was brilliant, or somebody around him was brilliant. I told him, 'That's the way to do it. Grab an image and make a statement.' "

Martin agrees. "Chris stands out in 'N Sync with the hair. I think if you always have one member that's a little bit off the wall . . . if you always have a Slash [from Guns 'N' Roses], that's almost a formula for all groups."

Just when 'N Sync thought they couldn't get any bigger, they released their second album, *No Strings Attached*. With hit songs like "Bye, Bye, Bye" and "This I Promise You" this record exceeded even the highest of expectations. In fact, the album surpassed all records by selling 1.1 million albums in its first day in release and 2.4 million albums within the first week. This is more than twice the number of albums sold by previous record holder the Backstreet Boys' *Millennium*.

With all the excitement surrounding their music career,

the guys have little time left to focus on anything else, like dating. "I've got a lot on my hands," JC told *Teen People*. "I got this gig running me ragged, and this is what I'm focused on. It's one thing to have an album do well, but it's another to create a career. And that's going to come from nothing but hard work and dedication."

In addition to performing on *No Strings Attached,* JC also produced four tracks on the album. His producing duties have begun to carry over to other recording artists. Most recently, JC produced several tracks for girl group Wild Orchid. "I figure, 'Okay, I'll bury my personal life for a good three, four years,' " JC admitted to *Teen People*. "You have to sacrifice, but tons of people do it."

But sacrifice is worth it if it makes their dreams come true. "From the beginning, we said, 'Let's be huge,' " Justin, who also produced one of the songs on *No Strings Attached,* told *Teen People*. "We didn't want to be the next *anybody*. We wanted to be the first 'N Sync."

And for those troublemakers who bring up the constant comparisons to another Orlando-based boy band, the guys don't let it bother them. "There's room enough for everybody," Joey said to *Teen People*.

"We don't look at anyone as rivals," Justin told the *London Free Press*. "I don't know if anyone looks at us as rivals. They're not really part of my world. I've got enough problems that I don't have to think about who doesn't like me. Our meetings have always been friendly and professional, so I can't say I feel like we're not appreciated."

There is no lack of appreciation for Chris, Joey,

Justin, JC, and Lance. Not from the fans, and not from each other. As Justin said so eloquently to the *London Free Press*, "I have faith, and as long as I'm with my four friends and we stick together, we will always be 'N Sync and there is no one who can hold us back."

Discography

Albums

'N Sync (European Debut CD) (BMG)

1. Tearin' Up My Heart
2. You Got It
3. Sailing
4. Crazy For You
5. Riddle
6. For The Girl Who Has Everything
7. I Need Love
8. Giddy Up
9. Here We Go
10. Best Of My Life
11. More Than A Feeling
12. I Want You Back
13. Together Again
14. Forever Young

'N Sync (BMG/RCA)

1. Tearin' Up My Heart
2. I Just Wanna Be With You
3. Here We Go
4. For The Girl Who Has Everything
5. God Must Have Spent A Little More Time On You

6. You Got It
7. I Need Love
8. I Want You Back
9. Everything I Own
10. I Drive Myself Crazy
11. Crazy For You
12. Sailing
13. Giddy Up

Home For Christmas (RCA)

1. Home For Christmas
2. Under My Tree
3. I Never Knew The Meaning Of Christmas
4. Merry Christmas, Happy Holidays
5. The Christmas Song (Chestnuts Roasting On An Open Fire)
6. I Guess It's Christmas Time
7. All I Want Is You This Christmas
8. The First Noel
9. In Love On Christmas
10. It's Christmas
11. O Holy Night (A Capella)
12. Love's In Our Hearts On Christmas Day
13. The Only Gift
14. Kiss Me At Midnight

Winter Album (BMG)

1. U Drive Me Crazy
2. God Must Have Spent A Little More Time On You
3. Thinking Of You
4. Everything I Own

5. Family Affair
6. Kiss Me At Midnight
7. Merry Christmas, Happy Holidays
8. All I Want Is You This Christmas
9. Under My Tree
10. Love Is In Our Hearts On Christmas Day
11. In Love On Christmas
12. The First Noel

No Strings Attached (Jive)
1. Bye, Bye, Bye
2. It's Gonna Be Me
3. Space Cowboy
4. Just Got Paid
5. It Makes Me Ill
6. This I Promise You
7. No Strings Attached
8. Digital Get Down
9. Bringin' Da Noise
10. That's When I'll Stop Loving You
11. I'll Be Good For You
12. I Thought She Knew

Singles

I Want You Back

Together Again

For The Girl Who Has Everything

U Drive Me Crazy

Tearin' Up My Heart

God Must Have Spent A Little More Time On You

Merry Christmas, Happy Holidays

Bye, Bye, Bye

Compilations

Sabrina, The Teenage Witch Soundtrack
(Universal/Geffen)
Giddy Up—'N Sync

Light It Up (Soundtrack) (Yab Yam Entertainment)
If Only In Heaven's Eyes—'N Sync

Music Of The Heart: The Album (Epic)
Music Of The Heart—'N Sync/Gloria Estefan
Music Of The Heart—'N Sync/Gloria Estefan (Pablo
Flores mix)

Web Site

www.nsync.com

Fan Clubs

'N Sync
P.O. Box 5248
Bellingham, Washington 98227

'N Sync
c/o Jive Records
137-139 West 25th Street
New York, New York 10001

Plus One

It's not the Four Seasons, but it may as well be. A five-story mansion overlooks private tennis courts, a swimming pool, and the beautiful Southern California coast. Just around the corner a recording studio sits amidst this sprawling multi-acre estate. Welcome to the home of record mogul David Foster, a fourteen-time Grammy Award-winning songwriter/producer who has worked with every artist from Barbra Streisand and Celine Dion to Brandy and 'N Sync. Tonight, a brand new band on the road to super-stardom gathers inside the studio, which is lined wall-to-wall with gold records, belting out what's sure to be the next big hit off their debut album.

Plus One is Christian music's answer to the Backstreet Boys—a boy band with a message and a whole lot of soul. While you may think that the group's name is a reference to Foster, their mentor, it actually goes much deeper than that, serving as a constant reminder

that spiritually, we are not alone. And while God may be the true leader of this band, the guys haven't been alone in the physical sense either since the group was formed almost a year ago. In fact, the five guys have been virtually inseparable: working, playing, and even living together.

Nathan Walters, the lovable big-brother type, shines as an amazing songwriter and incredible musician. His musical ability is matched only by Gabe Combs, the group's resident funny man. There's not a smile he can't crack or an instrument he can't play. Jeremy Mhire is the closest thing to a bad boy this group of altar boys has ever seen—but once he starts singing, you'll quickly forget he's ever been down a wrong path. Jason Perry, the baby of the group, is sure to make the girls swoon. The voice that booms from this heavenly hunk is powerful and beautiful. Nate Cole is the epitome of an angel. His musical ability and creative energy make him an invaluable asset to the band.

Jeremy and Gabe have just finished recording vocals on a cut called "My Friend." A short listening session ensues where the guys hear demos of songs they may potentially record. This is followed by a writing session where Nathan presents a song he's been working on. He strums his guitar while humming a melody. Nate and Jason harmonize impromptu. Even without lyrics, the song is pure magic. Talent really does exude from the room.

These luxurious surroundings are a far cry from the studio apartment the five young men first shared in San Francisco when the group was formed. Sharing close quarters was the perfect way to get these virtual

strangers on the fast track to bonding. After all, a year earlier, the individual members of Plus One were sprawled all over the country engulfed in their own personal lives. Dreams of becoming famous musicians hardly entered into their consciousness. Their biggest concerns were whether or not they'd be able to wake up in time for class, or who to ask to the school prom.

"It's weird. I don't even know why or how it all happened, but the first couple days we were together, we stayed up late and put everything on the table," says Nate. "I don't even know how comfortable I am with that because normally I wouldn't want to [reveal] everything, but I felt like I really didn't have anything to hide. We've had the same struggles and same experiences throughout life so I had no shame in saying what kinds of things I've gone through."

As a way of learning more about one another, the guys play a game where they challenge each other with hypothetical situations. Jeremy explains, "If you had to decide, would you rather have your arm chopped off and lemon juice poured in it, or have your ears cut off and never be able to hear the rest of your life?" It's not always far-fetched questions about gross anatomy, but you get the idea.

Perhaps playing this game helps them to better weigh the choices they are forced to make throughout life. Jason had to choose between finishing school and joining the group. "I was in my senior year of high school—the middle of football season, and [our manager] was telling me I have a week to get my life in order before I

move out of my house and away from everything that I've ever been around."

Joining the group has changed all of the guys' lives dramatically. The biggest jolt for the young quintet is learning to live on their own, away from parental supervision. "It's so weird because you're in that padding of your parents and your family, and your local church, and your school, and everything's just hunky-dory, and then bam—you're out in the world," explains Jason. "You have to figure out what you believe and why you believe what you do. You have to figure out who you are as a person."

"Now that I'm with the guys, we really rely on each other," says Nate. "There's no one that's making us wake up to go to church, there's no one to say you're punished if you do something wrong. We've been able to keep each other accountable, and encourage each other. I think we're gonna grow individually and teach ourselves to be disciplined. If we've got to sing the next day, we should not be staying up till two A.M."

At 21 Jeremy is one of the older members of the band and he's the only one who's really ever lived on his own before. "He's experienced a lot of things, and been around stuff that I haven't been around," says Nate. "I think it's good that he's in the group because he can relate to people who have experienced some of the same things. He will say, 'I've tried different things, but here I am and this is the better way it is to be.'"

Nathan is voted ladies man by the rest of the group. "He's a very good listener. Girls will love this in Nathan," says Nate. "I've seen him talk to a girl that

he's never met before, and I'll listen, and they're talking about deep stuff."

Jason adds, "He doesn't mess around with the small talk, he goes right for 'How's your relationship with God? Tell me about your childhood.' "

And like any great catch, Nathan isn't really looking for that special someone right now. "I know this sounds spiritual, but right now I'm not dating anybody and I don't want to. I just want to focus on what I'm doing," he reveals. "I think God will set me up. This is my mentality. As long as I'm seeking what God wants me to do, and being obedient to him, I think my path will cross with somebody at the right time. If it's premature, it's gonna mess things up because my focus is in the group."

Perhaps he has the right idea. After all, it takes a lot of work to perfect a musical act. For Plus One, it's so much more than singing, dancing, and looking good. These guys spend much of their time writing their own music. Unlike many of their contemporaries, the members of Plus One also play all of their own instruments.

Not to worry, it's not all work—the guys do break for fun. Among their hobbies are sports, movies, and shopping. Jason explains a typical adventure: "In *Dumb and Dumber* Jim Carrey rolls down the window and says, 'Excuse me, my limo driver's a bit lost. Can you help me?' We're in the car, and there's this hot girl next to us. Gabe rolls down the window and says, 'Excuse me. My driver's a bit lost.' We're in a two-door Accord!"

"He asked where the mall was," adds Nate. "We were right in front of the mall!"

If Plus One had to choose between getting their message across to a small select group of listeners, or achieving huge commercial success with a secular song, which would it be? Knowing this group, they won't ever have to make that decision. With God on their side, they'll accomplish both.

Discography

Album

The Promise
1. Written On My Heart
2. God Is In This Place
3. The Promise
4. My Life
5. Soul Tattoo
6. I Will Rescue You
7. When Your Spirit Gets Too Weak
8. Last Flight Out
9. I Run To You
10. Be
11. Here In My Heart
12. My Friend

Web Sites

www.143records.com/plusone

www.plusoneonline.com

Fan Club

Plus One
c/o 143 Records
530 Wilshire Boulevard, Suite 101
Santa Monica, California 90401

Youngstown

Hollywood Records is hidden away in the center of the Walt Disney Studio lot in Burbank, California. It's a long way from Youngstown, Ohio, where the label's newest act originated. Three guys lope into the conference room looking much more like the punk rockers of Blink 182 than the somewhat cleaned-up pretty boys that grace the cover of Youngstown's debut album *Let's Roll*. But a quick comparison with a framed poster of the group hanging on the wall reassures that these are indeed the same Midwestern trio.

Sitting amongst palm trees and movie stars is most shocking to the guys themselves. Just a few years back James Dallas, who goes solely by his last name, and David Yeager Jr., better known as DC, were in another band called Par Four. When three members of that band quit to pursue other interests, the guys met Sammy Lopez and the new trio started writing music together. "We still weren't calling ourselves a group," says

Dallas, the outspoken and unofficial leader of the band. "We could sing, we could harmonize, but it wasn't like we sat down every day and practiced and tried to do the group thing."

In fact, when a friend in Los Angeles called to offer the boys a record deal, the trio still didn't even have a name. "If our careers do last ten years from now, we can't be embarrassed by the name," explains Dallas, who suggested naming the group after the Ohio suburb where they first came together. But DC wasn't crazy about naming the band after the town where he had spent his entire life growing up.

"This is how history repeats itself," explains Dallas. "Everybody back in the day was using number names: All-4-One, Boyz II Men, etc. Before that were the seventies rock bands: Chicago, Boston, Kansas, etc. Nobody's got a city name today. Not only that, but it had meaning—that's where we met, that's where we put our thing together. It's where we didn't even decide to be a group, but for whatever reason it happened."

And it happened for them big time when the record company that signed them was part of the Disney empire. Without pause, the guys were folded into the Mouse House, pumping out the tunes "It's Not What You Think" for the Disney Channel's *The Famous Jett Jackson* and "I'll Be Your Everything" for Walt Disney Pictures' *Inspector Gadget*. They even had their own concert special, which debuted on the Disney Channel. Yet Sammy insists, "We still feel like the same kids that got the record deal a year ago."

Just because these boys are spending a lot of time at

Disneyland, doesn't mean that they've totally gone squeaky clean. "At first it was like they wanted clean-cut," reveals DC, slightly embarrassed by their earliest publicity photos. "Take out the piercings, cover the tattoos, etc. But then it kind of grew on them a little bit."

"People automatically think that we're these goody two-shoe kids—which we're not," explains Dallas. "We're not bad guys by no means, but we're normal guys. We like women. We like tattoos. We like piercings. I like rock music. I like rap music. I'm not a bad person. I'm not gonna look at some little kid and scream. At the same time, I'm not the type of person to walk around twenty-four/seven going [happy voice] 'Hi, Mickey.' "

More likely Dallas will walk around whistling while he works as he reveals the Disney character whom he's most like is Grumpy from *Snow White and the Seven Dwarfs*. "I wouldn't call me the grumpy guy, but I'm the first one to find the negative in the situation as opposed to the positive," he says. "I wear my heart on my sleeve, and my feelings get hurt a lot. Instead of sitting back and saying, 'You hurt my feelings,' I tend to snap back."

As for DC and Sammy, Goofy and Dopey most reflect their personalities, respectively. "Sammy always forgets everything and loses stuff," explains DC. "I'm on a [constant] sugar high."

Retaining their identity in this large family company isn't Youngstown's only challenge. They also face constant comparison with other boy bands. "I think it's a compliment when they compare us to Backstreet Boys

or 'N Sync or something like that," says DC. "Why would they come down on us? No one ever said, 'There's too many rock bands out there. There's too many rappers.' "

"It's up to you to decide whether or not you think we're different," says Dallas. "It's just a matter of whether or not you enjoy what we're doing, and whether or not we can entertain you. If anything makes us different, it's that we're not polished. It's not rehearsed. Naturally we rehearse to get onstage, but it's not so rehearsed that it becomes mechanical."

For anyone who has seen the guys in concert, you know that anything can happen. While performing in Flint, Michigan, Sammy decided to jump off the stage and hug a girl in the audience. "He didn't get a foot [offstage] and they snatched him," recalls Dallas. "He had his mike ripped right off his head."

"I'm looking at her while security's yanking her and pulling her face back," says Sammy. "She has my mike and I'm trying to grab it. Security pulls me back onstage and they give me my mike. I put it on right before my dance part comes on, and it's all crooked and beat up. She was crazy and I was scared."

But not all fan encounters are frightening. Sammy met one fan while performing in the Magic Kingdom and the encounter really stuck in his head. "She asked me a question that really just knocked me off my feet," says Sammy. "It gave me an opportunity to witness to her about what I have been through and what I know and hopefully that will help her and it did. She wrote me a letter and I was almost in tears when I read it. To

touch a person like that is greater than selling a million records really."

In fact, Youngstown tries to help their fans whenever possible, not only entertaining them with their music, but offering advice based on their own experiences growing up. Take Dallas, for instance: "Not to sound like a hypocrite, but the old saying that I wish I knew then what I know now is so true," reveals the one-time class clown. "Half the things that people do in school is to be popular, to be in that in crowd, and to be cool. When I am 100 percent myself, I am way cooler than I have ever been in my whole life.

"Back then, I was trying to hang out with the cool cats and I was drinking with them and skipping school. Deep down inside, my whole life, every time I would go to one of those parties, I didn't want to be there. Every time my boys would get some beer, I didn't want to do it. The one thing that I always did do, no matter how bad it got, when something real bad was getting ready to go down, I'd always dismiss myself from the situation. I'd be like, 'I'm tired, I'm gonna go home.'

"I think a lot of the problems that kids have is because not a lot of kids have the guts to tell that popular kid, 'I don't want to kick it with you tonight, you're doing stupid stuff.' But when you're twenty-five years old and you've got your own apartment, is this kid that you're trying to be cool with in high school gonna pay your rent? How you become this cool person is by working your butt off and accomplishing something that makes people respect you."

This type of work ethic is why Youngstown has

earned their share of respect. "We worked so hard for it," says DC. "It just feels good right here."

As the trio continues to roll forward, the future looks bright. With the success of the first album, and a live tour under their belt, Youngstown returns to their first love, doing what they do best, writing songs for their next album. "Ballads don't get dated, and that's pretty much what we write," says Dallas. "The ups, I like to leave that to everybody else because, what the hell . . . we're three white guys from the Midwest. It gets pretty corny."

Discography

Album

Let's Roll (Hollywood)
1. Pedal To The Steel
2. I'll Be Your Everything
3. Whenever You Need Me
4. Angel
5. Through Your Eyes
6. Forever In Love
7. The Prince You Charmed
8. Lose My Cool
9. Jamie Lee
10. Early Frost
11. Don't Worry
12. Remember
13. I'll Be Your Everything (from *Inspector Gadget*)
14. It's Not What You Think (from *The Famous Jett Jackson*)

Single

I'll Be Your Everything

Compilation

Inspector Gadget (Hollywood)
I'll Be Your Everything—Youngstown

Web Site

hollywoodrecords.go.com/youngstown/index.html

Fan Clubs

Youngstown
c/o Hollywood Records
170 Fifth Avenue, Ninth Floor
New York, New York 10010-5911

Youngstown
c/o Hollywood Records
500 South Buena Vista
Burbank, California 91521

Boy Bands around the Globe

We're clearly in the middle of a boy-band explosion. It seems as if new bands pop up every day. Not only in the United States but all over the world. This chapter briefly outlines several of the up-and-coming international guy groups you're sure to be hearing more about.

A1

With three Top-Ten U.K. singles within the same year from their debut album, *Here We Come,* A1 is already on their way to the top. Hit songs like "Be the First To Believe," "Summertime Of Our Lives," and "Every Time/Ready or Not" feature a blend of pop, funk, soul, and rock derived from the boys' own individual musical tastes. And why not? These impressive young lads actually wrote or cowrote every song on their album.

Christian Ingebrigtsen, Ben Adams, Paul Marazzi, and Mark Read make up A1. On the group's official

Web site, Christian addresses the whole boy-band phenomenon. "When you're doing photo shoots and tours for teen magazines, everyone perceives you as just another boy band," he says. "But when you're in the studio, the musicians and singers don't see you like that—to them you're musicians. Hopefully, we're getting that across to everyone else now, too."

Web site: **www.a1-online.com**

Another Level

Another Level came together in 1995 when Dane Bowers and Wayne Williams convinced Mark Baron and Bobak Kianoush to record a demo tape at a friend's recording studio. The demo eventually wound up in the hands of rapper Jay-Z, who signed the English group to his British record company, NorthWestSide Records. Since then this multicultural quartet has had four Top-Five UK singles from their self-titled debut album and recently opened for Janet Jackson's sold-out tour.

"This is not a copycat group," says Arista A&R V.P. Peter Edge to *Billboard*. "They have considerable teen appeal, but they're far more R&B-oriented than Backstreet Boys and the like. They're a self-formed group with a very strong point of view."

Unfortunately, the future of the band is presently unknown. At press time Wayne and Bobak have decided to leave the group to pursue other projects. Whether

Dane and Mark regroup and take the act to another level remains to be seen.

Web site: **www.anotherlevel.co.uk**

Area 4

The boy-band scene in Ireland is very interconnected. It started with a group called Up Front, which consisted of Ian Colgan, Danny O'Donaghue, and Mark Henderson. Mark left Up Front to join a new band, Men 2 B, alongside Farard Daver. Ian and Danny replaced Mark with Tommy Spratt and changed the name of their group to Frendz. Frendz didn't last very long and Danny joined a fledgling new group called Mytown (see page 169). In the meantime, Men 2 B were having problems of their own, and Mark was replaced by his newly available former bandmate, Ian. Two new members, John Collins and Roly Smithers, joined Farard and Ian, and the group's name was changed to Area 4. Farard left the band before the release of their debut album, and was replaced by seventeen-year-old Mark Cleary.

With the release of their first album, they're sure to give Boyzone a run for their money. The guys are all talented vocalists and dancers and bring a complementary blend of vocal styles to the group. They also all play instruments and write songs both individually and collectively.

Web site: **www.stevemartyn.com/area4.htm**

Code Red

Phil Rodell, Neil Watts, Roger Ratajczak, and Lee Misson grew up in the same neighborhood. Phil and Neil lived next door to each other, while the other guys lived just around the corner. No one could have predicted when the families first moved into their homes that their sons would grow up singing and form a successful band together.

"We were together a long time before we were signed to a record label," Roger told *All Stars*. But the boys' good looks, charisma, and catchy tunes caught the attention of a music manager who helped them secure a record deal.

When they were signed, the guys didn't have a name for their group. "When we were under Nicky [Graham, at Maximum Music], our private info was stored in a file that had a red color code for identification," Roger said in a *News Straits Times* interview. "Soon it was known as the 'code red' file, and we thought it sounded like a cool name. A mixture of danger and importance and we like it. So we kept the name and now you have . . . Code Red."

Positioned as a white British harmony group, Code Red's sound is influenced mostly by the black American sound. In fact, they've already covered Tevin Campbell's "Can We Talk" and Boyz II Men's "On Bended Knee." "We are not trying to be Boyzone, Take That, or 911," Roger said in a Hong Kong newspaper article. "On the contrary, we are singing R&B songs which sound like Damage, 3T, and Backstreet Boys."

And as far as these other boy bands go, Code Red would rather worry about themselves than so-called competition. "There's always competition," Phil told a Malaysian newspaper. "It doesn't really worry us too much because at the end of the day, if you're good enough, there's room for everybody."

fe3c

Better known as Steel, this band goes by fe3c, the chemical name for the metal. The reason the group chose this name is that it relates to their hard dance image. The trio that forms the group are G, Rich, and Ant. And while they may lack last names, they all sport nicknames a la the Spice Girls, reflecting their individual personalities.

Rich, better known as Surfer Steel, left school at sixteen after blowing up the physics lab. Accident prone Ant, or Sicknote Steel, has broken more than a dozen bones. And G, aka Student Steel, somehow managed to chop off his finger. The boys in this band lean toward the punk side as far as personalities go, but their sound is true boy-band material.

Web site: **www.fe3c.co.uk**

Human Nature

Hailing all the way from Australia, this awesome foursome took their debut album, *Telling Everybody,* to triple platinum status. Andrew Tierney, the group's founder, probably never imagined that they were des-

tined for success when he first brought his friends together to perform his personal arrangement of the classic tune "Earth Angel" at a high school concert.

Originally dubbed 4Trax, the guys got serious about their music and went to see Denis Handlin at Sony Music. Refusing to leave until he saw them, the quartet performed their single "People Get Ready," and they were signed on the spot.

These Down Under dudes have gone nowhere but up. Human Nature's second album, *Counting Down,* debuted in the number-one position on the Australian charts. Toby Allen, Phil Burton, and Michael Tierney, Andrew's younger brother, round out the band.

Web site: **www.humannature.com.au**

Mytown

This band first got together at the now defunct Digges Lane performing arts school in Dublin, Ireland. Member Marc Sheehan, who is also the group's choreographer, was teaching hip-hop dancing when he met Paul Walker, a former film and television actor. They dreamed of putting together a musical act and hooked up with Terry Daly, a graphic design student, and Danny O'Donoghue, who had been bouncing around the Irish music scene for a while (see Area 4, above).

Marc told *Seventeen* magazine that it's their closeness that gives them an edge over the competition. However, it may just be their talent that puts them over

the top. All the guys play instruments and write music. As for the name, it came to them one day as they sat atop a Dublin rooftop overlooking their hometown. For now, Mytown will have to rely on their memories as they spend a great deal of time away from home, touring the world, promoting their self-titled debut album. Their Irish eyes will be smiling as they climb the charts worldwide.

Web site: **www.mytown.ie**

911

In the early nineties, teenage dance fanatics Spike Dawbarn and Jimmy Constable met while working on England's late-night cult music show *The Hitman & Her*. The job took them to many cities including Carlisle, where the guys met Lee Brennan. The boys became fast friends once their mutual admiration for music was established, and 911 was born in 1995.

To date 911 has had nine U.K. top-ten hits including the number one single "Private Number." They've headlined two sellout U.K. tours, sold more than a million albums worldwide, and gone platinum six times in Southeast Asia. They've even released a greatest-hits album called *Greatest Hits & A Little Bit More*. A recent announcement on their Web site indicated that these British babes had decided to "pursue inivdual projects."

Web site: **c3.vmg.co.uk/911/index2.html**

2Be3

The French group 2Be3 are Frank Delhaye, Adel Kachermi, and Filip Nikolic. Filip and Adel grew up together in the same district of Paris. They met Frank in college and formed the band To Be Free with two other members, Judy and Sammy. After the other members split, in 1996, the trio regrouped and renamed themselves 2Be3.

Apparently, the boy bands in France feel the same way as the guy groups back home with regard to being labeled a "boy band." Filip told the *London Student*, "*Boy band* is not a term which applies to us. In France, it is a pejorative term which implies a prefabricated band."

Nonetheless, 2Be3's debut album, *Partir Un Jour*, went gold within two weeks of its release, becoming one of the best-selling records in France in 1997. The first two singles off that album landed simultaneously in the French Top Ten. These gorgeous *garçons* also star in their own sitcom on France's TF1 called *To Be Free* which centers around the lives of the band's three members before they made it big.

Web site: **www.2be3.com**

Westlife

Mark Feehily, Kian Egan, and Shane Filan were attending Summerhill College in Sligo, in the northwest of Ireland. They had just performed their final night of

the musical *Grease* when someone suggested they should form a musical act. They hooked up with three other guys and formed a band called 6 as 1. They managed to get together enough money to produce a CD single and they recorded "Together, Girl Forever" which actually got some airplay.

Louis Walsh, the manager of Boyzone, heard their song and got them a spot in the Backstreet Boys show when that band came to Ireland. From there, things started happening. The three other guys left the band and were replaced by Nicky Byrne and Bryan McFadden. They changed their name to IOU and signed contracts with Walsh. Ronan Keating, frontman for Boyzone, became co-manager with Walsh, and asked the guys to open for Boyzone's concert tour.

Once again the band changed names. This time they were to be known as Westside. However, it turned out that eight other bands were also using the name Westside, so the boys had to change their name yet again. This is when they finally settled on Westlife. Their debut single, "Swear It Again," raced to number one in Ireland and their album of the same name continues to perform well.

Web site: **www.westlife.co.uk**

Worlds Apart

In 1992, inspired by the success of New Kids on the Block, Gary Wilson arranged a casting call with the goal of producing a new boy band. Five young men

were chosen to be in the group Worlds Apart: Steve Hart, Patrick Osborn, Aaron Poole, Schelim Hannan, and Dan Bowyer. Their first album, *Together,* did not have much success. What's more, some of the members were jealous at the extra attention adorable Aaron was receiving.

Patrick left the group after the first year. He was replaced by Aaron Cooper, who decided to use his middle name Cal, to avoid confusion with the other Aaron. In 1994 both Dan and Aaron Poole decided to leave to pursue other interests.

Wilson contacted Nathan Moore, a former member of another group, Brother Beyond. Nathan had embarked on a solo career, but after much convincing, he joined Worlds Apart. This was a turning point for the band, and they released a second album, *Everybody,* which became diamond in 1996.

The next year Schelim left the group. He was replaced by Tim Fornara. Steve, Cal, Nathan, and Tim continue performing worldwide as Worlds Apart.

Stage and Screen

The boy bands are no longer limited by the constrictions of a CD or radio play. Faster than you can tell me the meaning of being lonely, guy groups are everywhere: live on stage, on the tube, and coming soon to a theater near you!

Boyband: The Musical

Thanks to the success of Take That and Boyzone, boy bands have always had a large following in the UK. Perhaps that is why it is in England where a musical about boy bands first debuted.

Boyband (one word), a live musical that features sixteen new songs, charts the ups and downs of five young lads who are thrust into the world of pop stardom. The play looks at the frustrations, tensions, success, and disappointments of being in a band. It focuses on the guys'

personal lives as well, including their personal struggles to remain in control of their lives.

The band depicted is called Freedom. Kevin Andrew, a Robbie Williams lookalike, plays Adam. Tom Ashton is shy boy Matt. Daniel Crossley portrays gritty Danny. Damien Flood is Sean. And Stepps (no last name) plays Jay.

The creative team behind the show is a most impressive collaboration. Writer/producer Steve Levine produced acts ranging from Culture Club to 911 and writer/producer Aron Friedman worked extensively with Take That on club mixes of their songs. Writer/producer Nicky Graham has worked with many music acts including Code Red. Emma Victoria, who choreographs 911, planned the moves for this stage show. The play itself was written by Peter Quilter.

While the play debuted to mediocre reviews, a tour is in the works. The show has also launched its own boy band onto the U.K. music scene. The cast has released a single as Brit Pack. Another case of art imitating life imitating art imitating . . . oh, never mind.

Dream Street

New York City is the home of one of the newest boy bands on the block. Dream Street, named after the Great White Way that is Broadway, comprises five card-carrying members of the actor unions, Equity and SAG.

Formed by Wall Street executive Brian Lukow and tap dancer Louis Baldonieri, the strategy behind Dream Street is to present a triple threat to the music business.

The group is already signed to a major record label, and they're currently in the process of putting together an entire Broadway show based around their first radio hit. The show is a made-up story involving the band's struggle to get started.

After auditioning hundreds of kids from the Broadway talent pool, Dream Street came together. There are five members in total. Matt Ballinger starred in *Sound of Music* and *The King and I*. Christopher Trousdale also starred in *Sound of Music*, as well as *Les Miserables*. Gregory Rapaso is best known for his performance at Graceland on the twentieth anniversary of Elvis's death. Frank Galasso played Martin Short's son in the film *Jungle 2 Jungle*. Jesse McCartney stars in the long-running soap opera *All My Children*.

Go Fatima

Have you ever wanted to impress your friends with the same fancy dance moves as today's hottest guy groups? Now you can when you watch *Go Fatima*, an easy-to-follow instructional video from the Backstreet Boys' very own resident choreographer, Fatima Robinson.

"We've grown with her from the first video," says AJ McLean. "We've all gotten tighter and better as dancers."

"They've just become better at everything they do," adds Fatima. "The boys first off are all just incredible singers, and the dancing just enhances their whole performance."

"She's worked with us from the beginning, and she's done all of our shows, everything we've done," explains Nick Carter.

Now Fatima can work with you, via your VCR, and teach you the secret steps behind Backstreet's "Everybody (Backstreet's Back)." And don't worry, if you don't get it all on the first try, just press rewind and try it again and again until you're a pro.

Jack of All Trades

Lou Pearlman and Trans-Continental have finally gone Hollywood with the debut of their first movie, *Jack of All Trades*. Based on an original idea by Pearlman, the story centers on brothers Jack and Alex Taylor, played by Tony DeCamillis and Joey Scolthrup, who find love and money in the world of big business. The story follows Jack, who with his best friend (Antonio Sabato, Jr.) has made a lot of money by entertaining lonely, rich women. When Jack is caught sleeping with one of his clients, her husband (Paul Sorvino) forces him to help steal a large sum of money by seducing a wealthy widow (Hunter Tylo). Ultimately, little brother comes to the rescue.

The most fascinating part of the entire film are the many cameo appearances by musical artists including: LFO, C Note, Phoenix Stone, Mista Brizz, Britney Spears, 'N Sync, and many more. "Joey and JC work at a pizzeria," reveals Lionel C. Martin, director of the film and numerous music videos. "Justin plays the car valet. Chris is in the pizzeria, too, but he's a patron.

Lance plays a flight navigator. Britney Spears is the flight attendant. It's a good fun movie that's aimed at that same market that [Lou's] selling all these records to."

And, as expected, the soundtrack rocks. "Well, we do have some experience in that business," claims Pearlman. "We do have a brand-new, unreleased 'N Sync song, and a brand-new, unreleased LFO song." There will also be songs from most of the other groups making cameo appearances in the film.

Look for more family synergy behind the scenes. Robert Fischetti, one of the film's executive producers, is the brother of LFO's Brad Fischetti. After all, Disney World is not the only small world in Orlando these days.

Making the Band

Part of ABC's famous TGIF lineup, *Making the Band* takes the basic genre of following real people and creating drama from the structure of their lives and applies this formula to a brand-new boy band. "We're basically taking what we learned from the *Real World*, and even later when we did *Road Rules*, where we followed a cast on a series of missions," says John Murray, co-executive producer of the new show, and co-creator of *Real World* and *Road Rules*. "In a sense, this is one big mission: Make a band."

"The structure for this is quite different," notes Mary-Ellis Bunim, Murray's partner on all of their shows. "This has its own unique structure of putting

together twenty-five people and then culling them down to eight, and finally to five members of a band."

The task of actually putting the new band together was delegated to Lou Pearlman, the genius behind such bands as Backstreet Boys, 'N Sync, and LFO. Pearlman, who describes the show as *"Real World meets The Monkees meets Backstreet Boys,"* looked at manufacturing a band for TV as a new challenge.

"It's my first time really doing an open audition," says Pearlman. "I've always had people who kind of knew people come to me. This is taking a total risk, going out there, trying to find guys that would like each other, get to know each other, get along with each other, and be able to sing in harmony."

After endless casting calls in cities all across America, five boys made it into the band that has come to be known as O-Town. Ashley Parker Angel, from Redding, California, was introduced to music at age four when his mom first taught him how to play the piano. Erik-Michael Estrada, from New York City, is an avid songwriter and extremely proud of his part Puerto Rican descent. Ikaika Kahoana, from Honolulu, Hawaii, left behind his pre-med studies to follow his passion for entertaining like the rest of his family. Trevor Penick, from Fullerton, California, half African American, half white, was a theater major before joining the group. Jacob Underwood, from San Diego, California, has always dreamed of becoming a rock star.

"To put it all together was a feat in itself, to let alone record some songs and to get it all together in the time element that we would need for a TV show," says

Pearlman. "For me it was something like, on a mini-scale, going to the moon and back, given the time element you have."

"Lou Pearlman has an important influence in the course of events of this series," notes Bunim. "He is a major decision maker when it comes to choosing this band and guiding their career paths, choosing material for them to record, and so whether or not he's physically present in a lot of scenes in the episodes, his presence is certainly felt throughout."

"He has done everything he can in terms of putting this together to make sure that this band is gonna be successful as a band first and foremost," adds Murray. "When we first talked to Lou Pearlman, he initially said, 'This couldn't make a better series because whenever I've done these bands, there's so much natural drama that happens. We always end up with someone who for one reason or another quits the band. We always end up with someone who has major problems with their girlfriend because the band becomes a family and the girlfriend feels left out, or even more so when the boy becomes famous, how does it effect the hometown girlfriend relationship.

"There's so many things," Murray continues. "There's the vying for leadership within the band. There are so many issues that come up because everyone involved is so passionate. There are issues over some of the guys who will be writing music and whether or not Lou wants to use that music as part of the band, and the tension over that. So there are just so many naturally dramatic things that occur in putting a band together."

And will O-Town eventually reach the same level of worldwide success as Pearlman's other groups? "We don't know what they can do," says Pearlman. "We hope they can meet the levels of an 'N Sync, an LFO, or even a Backstreet, but certainly that's up to the group, and my mission here was putting together a group for TV. So who knows what will happen? We hope for the best. We're giving them the same talent ability. We have our studio facilities, our vocal coaches, and choreographers that will work with them to cultivate their talents, but certainly it's gonna be up to them to pull it off."

Adds Murray, "For people like me, who didn't know that much about it, and saw it initially as just a bunch of pretty faces who are put through a factory, I think you learn that these are musicians, they do write a lot of their own music, and a lot of hard work goes into doing what they do."

2Gether

2Gether was the first ever original made-for-television movie to air on MTV. What better subject matter for MTV's first foray into film than boy bands? It's a spoof to end all spoofs, poking fun at the hype surrounding today's youth-dominated pop music scene as well as directing many specific jabs at those leading managers, producers, and performers who make it all happen.

"It's about dreams," explains the film's director, Nigel Dick, who has much experience in the world of

teen music himself, having directed videos for Backstreet Boys, 'N Sync, and many other young acts. "It's about a manager who manages a band, like Backstreet Boys or 'N Sync, and he starts questioning who he is and what it is he does, and then he stumbles upon this talent and he decides to form another band and have another crack at it. He finds five kids, and he's got seven days to get a band together and do a gig. He puts them together and makes something out of nothing and resurrects himself."

The group's manager, Bob Buss, is played masterfully by Alan Blumenfeld, an actor who looks suspiciously like Lou Pearlman. All the guys in the band have various dreams. Evan Farmer plays Jerry O'Keefe, the heartthrob. Alex Solowitz is rebel Mickey Parke. Jason "Q.T." McKnight, the Nick Carter/Justin Timberlake type, is played by Michael Cuccione. Chad Linus, the shy one, is portrayed by Noah Bastian. Kevin Farley, Chris Farley's brother, comedically plays the reassuring older-brother type, Doug Linus. "They do their own singing and dancing," notes Dick.

"There are archetypes in the band," says Dick. "We start right off in the first five minutes, the manager says, 'Look, there's five types in the boy band: You've got your reassuring older brother type, your mascot, the heartbreaker, the shy one, and the bad boy.' If I was making *Full Metal Jacket 2*, I would be doing a story about guys in the infantry going to battle, and I'd need five archetypes: the spectacled one frightened of going into battle, the macho one without his sleeves on his shirt and the big machine gun, the Black one from the

ghetto, etc. Whatever story you tell, you'll come up with five types."

Do today's bands mind being parodied? "We talked to a number of bands about it because we were trying to get them to be in it, but they all turned us down," concedes Dick. "It's like [*This Is*] *Spinal Tap* [a 1984 mockumentary spoofing heavy metal bands]. When *Spinal Tap* came out, I was in England and I went to the first screening, which was attended by members of Def Leopard and Iron Maiden, and all the rest of it. Their initial reaction was they were really pissed off. Not because it was slagging their particular type of music, but because they were all individually convinced that somebody in their group, or one of their ex-roadies, had flown to California, tracked down [director] Rob Reiner, and told him their life story.

"If you have ever played in a band, you have played the air force gig, you have met that woman from the record label who is totally two-faced. Because there are situations in our film that could be perceived as knocking 'N Sync or Backstreet Boys, whatever, the truth of it is I didn't approach the movie from that point of view, I approached the movie from a point of view, this is what happens to a band on the road, and of course you inflate it to make it more interesting in the story. And it's true of virtually any group, you turn up, do a gig, you suck. You get bottled off stage. We've all gone through that. You try to do something interesting visually, and it backfires upon you—the Stonehenge moment. There's a Stonehenge moment in our movie. I'm sure every band has been through that. You're Pink Floyd and

you're doing *The Wall,* and the wall won't fall down. I think that's true of any theatrical endeavor."

2Gether definitely holds up. Fans of boy bands watched the movie's premiere in droves, paying homage to the boys and the bands they love so much. At press time Pearlman hadn't seen the film himself. He was at a KC and the Sunshine Band concert when the movie initially aired. However, due to the movie's incredible ratings, he'll have another chance to check out this boy band's adventures when they return later this year as a weekly series on MTV.

The Future of
Boy Bands

The big debate remains: Is this boy-band phenomenon a fad, or are these guy groups here to stay? If history serves as an example, these acts will eventually phase out over time only to be replaced by some other trend in music. After a long absence from the scene, a new generation of boy bands will appear with their own unique traits.

But forget history for a moment. Examine the current state of the music business. These bands show no signs of going away. In fact, they're getting stronger and multiplying. They're no longer a small segment of the music industry, they're dominating the record business. Recent sales figures on albums and concert tickets for the Backstreet Boys and 'N Sync are unmatched by any other musicians—ever.

The only end to this era of boy bands will be induced by the guys themselves. Jive Records recently announced that they were planning solo projects for many

of the individual members of Backstreet Boys and 'N Sync. Will these two megabands follow in the footsteps of Boyzone, with solo albums and other projects taking time and energy away from performing as a group?

As this book goes to print, Backstreet Boy AJ McLean tours to sold-out venues as solo performer Johnny No-Name. Nick Carter is drawing a comic book based on the band with legendary artist Stan Lee. Howie D. has signed to star in a movie. 'N Sync's Justin Timberlake has already done a film for the Disney Sunday Movie called *Model Behavior*. Can more acting roles be far behind? Meanwhile, his bandmates are equally busy with their own individual projects. JC Chasez is producing songs for other bands. Lance Bass has started his own management firm representing several successful country acts.

Perhaps the diversification of these bands will allow their competitors access to the top of the charts. No Authority has high hopes for their follow-up album. Hanson and the Moffatts are both crossing over into broader musical genres, vastly increasing their fan bases. MDO's upcoming English album will introduce these Latin performers to a whole new market that is bound to increase their visibility in the States.

As long as there are fans to buy the music and go to the concerts, boy bands will continue to flourish. Perhaps you will grow old, change your musical tastes, and these albums will begin to collect dust. Somehow, you'll never be able to throw them out, give them away, or sell them on e-bay. They'll become a guilty pleasure

down the road. Once a year you'll listen to your CDs and they'll bring you back to a simpler time, conjuring up images of first loves, happy occasions, and many special memories.

Years from now you'll try to share this music with your own children, and you'll never quite understand why Nick and Justin don't take their breath away, like they did yours at their age. Perhaps you'll have déjà vu and tell your own parents that you finally understand their strange obsession with David Cassidy and Donny Osmond. Your kids will also have a new set of teen idols whose every move they worship. You'll support their habit, buy them the albums, and even accompany them to concerts, developing your own guilty crushes on your daughters' fantasy boys.

There will always be a place for boy bands in our hearts and dreams. We'll always have the music, and the memories. I offer this advice to the fans and the bands: Don't worry about what's to come. Don't think about who may or may not be around tomorrow. Just enjoy it while it lasts, because it won't last forever. Give it your all. Most important, have fun.

Additional Web Sites

Nigel Dick
www.nigeldick.com/index.html

Full Force
www.angelfire.com/ny3/FULLFORCE

Irish Pop
www.irishpop.co.uk

Jive Records
www.peeps.com/jiverecords/index.html

New Kids on the Block
www.nkotb.com

Radio Disney
disney.go.com/RadioDisney

Fatima Robinson
www.gofatima.com

Trans-Continental Entertainment
www.t-con.com

JoJo Wright
www.jojowright.com

About the Author

FREDERICK LEVY wrote this book because he wanted to see free concerts and gain backstage access to meet his favorite bands. He's not only a fan of pop music, he's fascinated by the whole boy-band phenomenon. When he's not listening to his growing CD collection, he can be found cruising through Los Angeles in his Mustang convertible.

Levy is the vice president of Marty Katz Productions. Since joining the company in 1994, he has been involved in such films as *Man of the House* (1995), starring Jonathan Taylor Thomas, for Walt Disney Pictures; *Mr. Wrong* (1996), starring Ellen DeGeneres, for Touchstone Pictures; *Titanic* (1997), starring Leonardo DiCaprio, for Paramount Pictures and Twentieth Century-Fox; *Reindeer Games* (2000), starring Ben Affleck, and *Impostor* (2000), starring Gary Sinise, both for Dimension Films.

Levy started his career as a guest coordinator on the TV show *Love Connection*. He also worked in professional radio as creator/producer of *Then & Now* and *The Celebrity DJ Party*. Born in Massachusetts, he is a graduate of the University of Southern California where he earned a degree in business. Today he teaches film classes at the Los Angeles branch of Emerson College, UCLA-Extension, and USC's School of Cinema-

Television. He is a regular speaker on the lecture circuit and has been a guest on hundreds of TV and radio talk shows.

Levy's first book, *Hollywood 101: The Film Industry*, a *Los Angeles Times* bestseller, is an entertaining and informative guide to making it in Hollywood. *The Ultimate Boy Band Book* is Levy's second book. Correspondence to the author can be sent in care of this publisher or directly by e-mail to **author@boybandbook.com**. Readers can visit his Web site at **www.boybandbook.com**.

DON'T MISS ANY OF OUR
BESTSELLING POP MUSIC BIOS!

DARK SECRETS™
by Elizabeth Chandler

Who is Megan? She's about to find out....
#1: Legacy of Lies

Megan thought she knew who she was.

Until she came to Grandmother's house.

Until she met Matt, who angered and attracted her as no boy ever had before.

Then she began having dreams again, of a life she never lived, a love she never knew...a secret that threatened to drive her to the grave.

Home is where the horror is....
#2: Don't Tell

Lauren is coming home, eight years after her mother's mysterious drowning. They said it was an accident. But the tabloids screamed murder. Aunt Jule was her only refuge, the beloved second mother she's returning to see. But first Lauren stops at Wisteria's annual street festival and meets Nick, a tease, a flirt, and a childhood playmate.

The day is almost perfect—until she realizes she's being watched.

A series of nasty "accidents" makes Lauren realize someone wants her dead.

And this time there's no place to run....

Archway Paperbacks
Published by Pocket Books

3027

Don't Miss a Single Play!

Archway Paperbacks Brings You the Greatest Games, Teams, and Players in Sports!

By

Bill Gutman

☆Football Super Teams

☆Bo Jackson: A Biography

☆Michael Jordan: A Biography (revised)

☆Baseball Super Teams

☆Great Quarterbacks of the NFL

☆Tiger Woods: A Biography

☆ Ken Griffey, Jr.: A Biography

☆ Brett Favre: A Biography

☆Sammy Sosa: A Biography

☆Shaquille O'Neal: A Biography (revised)

 An Archway Paperback
Published by Pocket Books

630-13

No Authority

911

Youngstown

Barry Talesnick/Retna

LFO

Ilpo Musto/London Features

Boyzone

Westlife

Jeffrey Mayer/Star File

The Moffatts

Jeffrey Mayer/Star File

98 Degrees

5ive

BBMak

Johnny Buzzerio

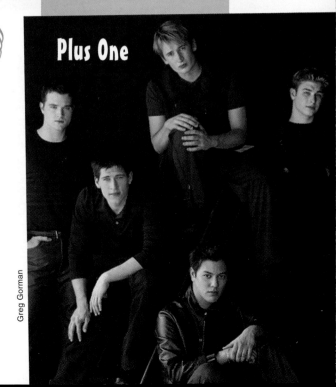

Plus One

Greg Gorman

'N Sync

Backstreet Boys

John Gladwin/Retna

Jeffrey Mayer/Star File

David Atlas/Retna

♪ **C Note**

MDO